LET THERE BE NIGHT

LET THERE BE NIGHT

TESTIMONY ON BEHALF OF THE DARK

PAUL BOGARD, EDITOR

UNIVERSITY OF

NEVADA PRESS

RENO

LAS VEGAS

For my mother and father
who introduced me to the night

University of Nevada Press, Reno, Nevada 89557 USA
Copyright © 2008 by University of Nevada Press
All rights reserved
Manufactured in the United States of America
Design by Kathleen Szawiola

LIBRARY OF CONGRESS CATALOGING-IN-PUBLICATION DATA
Let there be night : testimony on behalf of the dark /
Paul Bogard, editor. — 1st ed.
    p. cm.
Includes bibliographical references and index.
ISBN 978-0-87417-328-4 (pbk. : alk. paper)
1. Urban ecology. 2. Municipal lighting. 3. City and town life.
I. Bogard, Paul, 1966–
HT241.L48 2008
307.76—dc22   2008016525

The paper used in this book is a recycled stock made from 30 percent
post-consumer waste materials, and meets the requirements of American
National Standard for Information Sciences–Permanence of Paper for
Printed Library Materials, ANSI/NISO Z39.48-1992 (R2002). Binding
materials were selected for strength and durability.

Credits: "A Backyard History of Light," by Christopher Cokinos, first
appeared in *Turnrow,* Winter 2007, copyright © 2007 by Christopher
Cokinos. "In Praise of Darkness," by John Daniel, first appeared in
Southwest Review, Fall 2007, copyright © 2007 by John Daniel. "Why
the Night Sky Is Dark," from *An Intimate Look at the Night Sky* by Chet
Raymo. Reprinted by permission of Walker & Company. Excerpts from
"Earth's Body" from *Staying Put* by Scott Russell Sanders. Copyright
© 1993 by Scott Russell Sanders. Reprinted by permission of Beacon
Press, Boston.

FIRST PRINTING
17 16 15 14 13 12 11 10 09 08
5 4 3 2 1

Our fantastic civilization has fallen out of touch with many aspects of nature, and with none more completely than with night . . .

With lights and ever more lights, we drive the holiness and beauty of night back to the forests and the sea . . .

HENRY BESTON, "Night on the Great Beach,"
from *The Outermost House* (1928)

CONTENTS

LET THERE BE NIGHT

INTRODUCTION: WHY DARK SKIES?

PAUL BOGARD

When I think of dark nights, I think of this lake in northern Minnesota. On the longest day of the year, my father and I watch as the sun sets across the water and night begins filling a clear sky. Soon the Summer Triangle stands directly over us, Scorpio rises from the bay to our left, and the Big Dipper emerges high above where the sun has set. I ask my father, deeply involved in organizing property owners around the lake to resist the ever-increasing pressure from developers, if he has ever considered a dark-sky ordinance.

"What's a dark-sky ordinance?"

The answer is easy enough—laws regulating the use of artificial lighting—and difficult enough that I am soon stumbling, wanting to say, *Dad, it's about holiness and beauty, shouldn't that be enough?* and knowing that in the world today, it is not. I know the question my father is really asking, the question anyone would ask: why? Why would we need a dark-sky ordinance? Or more specifically, why dark skies?

My answer begins in this place where my parents built a cabin the year I was born. I grew up coming here every summer, and every summer the dark, starry skies over the lake deepened their impression on me.

It is still quite dark here, and on calm midnights I often take our ancient aluminum canoe out among the stars. I paddle slowly, pulling myself toward the center of the lake, looking back to see the house receding through steam, the smooth water warmer than air. A barred owl calls from dark shoreline, loons from the south bay. A bat flickers by, bits of leaves and broken bugs mix with stars in still water, a handful of amber cabin lights linger in the pines. I lean back on the bow and the Milky Way bends above me, one horizon to the other, there as it has always been.

As a child I was afraid of night at the lake because the dark was so thick it seemed tangible, something you could stick your hands into or hold, like muck, or drapery. And the woods are still that way, but the sky is beginning to wear at the edges where gas stations hope to attract customers by immolating themselves in white light, and roadside restaurants blow their electricity bills straight into the sky. Each summer when I return to the lake I am no longer so much afraid of the dark as I am afraid for the dark.

I fear that the holiness and beauty Henry Beston saw being driven from his nights on Cape Cod some eighty years ago are now being driven from mine. It is this fear that inspired me to collect the essays that together make *Let There Be Night: Testimony on Behalf of the Dark.*

·.·

We are losing dark skies all over the globe, but nowhere more than in western Europe and North America. Astronomers say that because of light pollution, fully 80 percent of the people living in these areas no longer experience "real night," that is, real darkness. The night most of us know is no longer what it was. And the costs are high.

We are wasting hundreds of millions of dollars a year, for one thing. Besides creating light pollution, poorly designed lighting, whether in amount or fixtures or both, adds unnecessary costs to our light bills.

We are endangering ourselves and wasting money attempting to improve our safety. Poorly designed streetlights and store signs send glare directly into drivers' eyes; poorly lit sidewalks and doorways provide shadows for those we seek to avoid. In matters of safety, it is far more important that lighting be effectively used than abundantly used.

We are ignoring the warnings from scientists who increasingly report the connection between serious disease and our addiction to light at night. Our bodies have evolved in bright days and dark nights, and need one as much as the other. Attempting to do without the latter seems to have serious consequences for our physical health.

These are real costs—an argument using only such reasons alone ought to convincingly answer my father's question. And yet there are other costs, costs that are harder to quantify than those financial ones our culture understands.

It is easy to forget that we humans are not the only species to suffer the costs of light pollution. Night is when the wild earth comes alive. An example that stands out to me is how more than four hundred species of songbirds migrate at night across North America, and how whatever internal compass they have used for however many millions of years is confused by our bright spills. How hundreds of thousands of birds every year are killed by our lights, either from being drawn toward and colliding with structures or from circling the light until they drop from exhaustion.

The list of nocturnal (or crepuscular—active at dawn and dusk) birds, animals, amphibians, and insects is long, and each species has had millions of years not only to adapt to darkness but to come to depend on it. Some are as famous as wolves and sea turtles, some as ignored as salamanders and moths. As we allow the light from our buildings and roadways to devour the darkness, we threaten these lives. The "cost" to them as we invade their dark world is obvious, and reason enough to stop our advance. But think too of how they help shape our experience. How can we understand what it means to lose their presence from our lives?

In his Journal from March 23, 1856, Henry David Thoreau lamented the diminishing of nature by those who had come before him. "I hear that it is but an imperfect copy that I possess and have read, that my ancestors have torn out many of the first leaves and grandest passages, and mutilated it in many places. I should not like to think that some demigod had come before me and picked out some of the best of the stars. I wish to know an entire heaven and an entire earth." Whenever I read this I think "me too." To imagine the night sky before light pollution is to feel cheated. To then imagine that because of our ignorance and inaction our children won't see what we have seen is worse.

I think again of the "beauty" and "holiness" of Henry Beston's night. The sight of stars and planets; the sound of loons, owls, wolves; the scent of pine, lake water, wood smoke—my senses tell me that the lake's night is still an example of beauty that would be evident to us all. But what of night's "holiness"?

My dictionary is of no help at first, offering only a stiff "exalted or worthy of complete devotion as one perfect in goodness and righteousness." And so I think of Thoreau's words, and that holiness must come in part from wholeness. For night, that means "an entire heaven" unblemished by light pollution, "an entire earth" still home to the steps and calls of nocturnal and crepuscular creatures. I think of a darkness so deep you can't see your outstretched hands; a night so dark that the phrase "dark night of the soul" still has the power and meaning it did for the sixteenth-century Spanish monk St. John of the Cross. I think of a sky so free of pollution that you feel as though you might fall into its three dimensions, a sky so plush with stars that "snowstorm" is your first thought as you step out under it, a sky so brilliant you can't help but wonder about a force greater than yourself. And farther down the page my dictionary admits that "holy" can also mean "venerated as or as if sacred."

What would happen if we were to understand darkness as sacred?

We would turn down our lights, for one thing. We would design our fixtures so they sent no light into the sky. We would understand that the wildness upon which the places we love depend, depends itself on the darkness of night.

We would understand that the answer to the question, Why dark skies? is as easy as because we are wasting enormous sums of money and endangering the lives of those we love, and as difficult as speaking of holiness and beauty—how as we lose "real night" we lose an opportunity to bring into our lives these invaluable qualities.

We would float under stars imagining the night we knew as a

child, the night we may know in the future, and would do whatever we could to ensure there be little difference between them.

·✦·

In a world full of problems that can seem beyond our grasp, stopping the spread and effects of light pollution offers an opportunity we don't often get: a serious environmental problem we—each of us individually, and all together—can do something about.

I sometimes think that if we could just get enough people to experience night as it once was, the problem of light pollution would quickly be tackled. In *Let There Be Night,* I've asked twenty-nine writers to help. To raise awareness of what we're losing as we are losing night. To help us understand what we could bring back into our lives. It is a way of asking them to share their experience of real night, to hear their answers to the question, why dark skies?

"I'm writing to you with night in mind," my letter to each writer began. I asked for "a story, a meditation, a reflection, but somehow a testimony for the value of night—real night, dark night, wild night—and a statement against the loss of night to artificial night lighting."

"As you may know," I wrote, "the light pollution blocking our view of the stars is only the most obvious result of artificial night lighting. Our lack of attention to the spread of these lights mirrors a lack of appreciation for night's ancient gifts of quiet, peace, and time to be with those we love. And, perhaps most seriously, as we've diluted the darkness, so have we negatively affected ecosystems in ways we're only beginning to understand."

I wrote of my vision for a book that would inspire and support citizens, legislators, and organizations as they argued for a clear view of the night sky, the importance of darkness for the world's ecosystems, and the balancing of safety concerns with the needs of nocturnal species. I shared my optimism that while artificial night lighting—light pollution—continues to spread, so too is awareness of its negative effects spreading. I presented my intention to donate any royalties from sales of the book to support groups actively and effectively working on behalf of the night.

I have always wanted *Let There Be Night* not only to offer an urgent call to awareness and action but also to serve as a statement of hope—many of the negative effects of artificial night lighting can be diminished, even halted and reversed, simply by reducing or eliminating our use of artificial lights. One good example of this: once you become aware of light pollution, you see it everywhere. So many of our lights are unshielded—meaning the light sprays in all directions, including into our eyes and into the sky. Simply by insisting our lights be shielded, we could significantly improve safety by eliminating glare and improve our view of the stars by reducing the light shining into the sky.

·_*·

In *Let There Be Night* no one style dominates, and essay lengths vary from eight hundred to four thousand words. I like that. I wanted there to be shorter essays for reading aloud around a campfire or in bed before falling asleep, and longer essays for immersing in the writer's voice and subject. Each writer was free to approach the assignment as he or she desired, and I hope the balance between these approaches—in style, in length—makes for a pleasant and inspiring read, whether from cover to cover or by picking an essay here and another there.

The essays are divided among five sections, each section centered on a theme that is itself an argument for the value of night's natural darkness. While the sections organize the essays, their borders are permeable—each of the essays could fit in more than one of the sections—and the five section themes reflect only a handful of the possible arguments. The book closes with its sole interview, in which Christian Luginbuhl of the U.S. Naval Observatory in Flagstaff offers a view of "What the Solution Would Look Like."

One of the challenges of an anthology is that it is impossible to include all worthy voices. As such, while *Let There Be Night* includes contributions from writers in many diverse locations, it is not meant to be exhaustive. All over the world, in every culture, there would be voices with appreciation of night's darkness to share. I hope this collection helps to bring those voices forward, to strengthen with their harmonies the chorus calling for awareness and change.

Every summer night, when not canoeing after the moon, I sit on our screened-in porch in a great corner chair and read. Reading and night have gone together for me since I was a child and my parents sat on the edge of my bed with stories. Just as those bedtime books—*Make Way for Ducklings, Swimmy, A Snowy Day,* and many others—offered me an invitation to the world of reading, I hope *Let There Be Night* offers an invitation to explore this other half of our life, the time and place we call night.

I like to imagine readers taking this collection to their own favorite nighttime roost, somewhere with an amber light to shade the darkness, somewhere with stars close by, somewhere with the scents and sounds of darkness. I like to imagine them walking outside, seeing night in a new way for the first time.

PART ONE

SPIRIT

What does darkness mean to the human spirit? In "The Gifts of Darkness," Kathleen Dean Moore cites a sense of connection with creation, and argues that when night's darkness is dimmed or destroyed by artificial light, we shut children off "from fully half the human experience of what is wonderful." Thomas Becknell echoes Moore in "Old Hymns of the Night" when he writes of how "millions of children grow up never having seen the night sky," and how because of "our earthly lights . . . we are losing a sense of holiness and beauty and mystery." In "Trespassing on Night," David Gessner offers the story of one community fighting back on behalf of darkness, and speaks of the way night's darkness can "work on you in a way that isn't easily put into words." Putting the meaning of such things as solitude, awareness, and "mental and spiritual wholeness" into words is exactly what John Daniel explores in his essay "In Praise of Darkness." He asks, "Who can say what we are losing?" as we lose the night. "The loss is more than aesthetic," claims Susan Hanson in "Deep in the Heart." For Hanson the loss has to do with "the desire to know God," and how our ability to know God is diminished with the diminishment of darkness. And finally, in "Nocturnes," Laurie Kutchins claims night as "the cradle for magic, mystery, and love."

THE GIFTS OF DARKNESS

KATHLEEN DEAN MOORE

We sat by a woodstove in a lean-to shelter in the Cascade Mountains. Snow had fallen all day, but the skies had cleared at nightfall. Susan and I looked out into a Milky Way so densely packed with stars that it might have been a snowdrift. The snowdrifts themselves might have been the Milky Way, snow-ice blinking in blue shadows. Tips of hemlock trees rolled like fiddleheads under the weight of glowing snow. We talked about Cassiopeia and infinite distance. We talked about children.

"I took my niece to the planetarium in St. Louis last week," Susan told me. I looked up at the angry edge in her voice. "I had told her we could do anything she wanted that day, but that's what my niece wanted most—to show me the stars." Susan leaned back against the wall and stared at her gloved hands.

"After the star show was over, you know what that little girl said? I'll never forget it. She said, 'Aunt Susan, did you know that a long time ago, people could see stars like this?' She wanted me to believe her. She said, 'Really. Once there were that many stars in the sky, and people could just look up, and there they were! Right there. In the sky.'"

Susan shoved a log into the firebox and clanked the door closed. "How could she know any different? In a way, she's right—there aren't many stars left in her life."

·.*

What do we take away from a child, I wondered then, when we take the starlight and give her instead a planetarium and the blinding, floodlit city? Or put the question the other way: What are the gifts that darkness gives?

I think first of the gift of mystery. Artificial light makes it difficult to see beyond our constricted, human-centered world. A child might be forgiven for thinking that's all there is. But when we douse the lights, a child can discover that the universe is lit by lamps humans did not switch on, deepened by distances we cannot fathom, moved by forces we do not understand.

Mystery opens the human spirit to what is beyond it. Encountering that mystery gives a person a sort of "night vision" of the imagination. Night vision, the ability to see in the dark, is strengthened by darkness, and quickly destroyed by light. And isn't this true of imagination as well, nourished by mystery and diminished by the glare of certainty and human pride?

But there's more. Darkness feeds a sense of wonder, a young person's great gift—astonishment at a world alive with marvels. The world is half the time in darkness; this is a fact of the great spinning Earth. When we protect children from darkness, when we dim or destroy it with artificial light, we shut them off from fully half the human experience of what is wonderful. When we limit children to those worlds they can see, we risk closing them to worlds they can only hear or smell or feel against their skin. This is an offense against exhilaration and joy. Blessed is the person who holds a childhood memory of that first night sleeping in the backyard—the heavy dew, the smell of mown grass, headlights sweeping the hedges, crickets suddenly still.

And so, finally, this: A third gift of darkness is a more intimate connection with the natural world. When light falls away and darkness comes on, when killdeer fall silent and the hedgerows begin to breathe, when stars blink on, only Arcturus and Aldebaran at first, then the whole wash of the Milky Way, when the wind stills as the moon rises; then the structure of the built world begins to vanish. The boundaries of the body fade into darkness. Then a child might feel herself truly part of the night. This kinship is an ancient comfort, the embrace of the extended family of living things. And from this deeper connectedness can come a deeper caring for all the plants and animals and children, all of us together in this one infinite night, breathing the exhalation of elderberries and damp earth.

·*·

Many years ago, we carried our son into a cave in the mountains, farther and farther into darkness. I don't remember how old he was—one year? two?—but I remember his excitement. "When we get to the grotto," we told him, "we'll give you your own flashlight, so you can see," and I don't know if he was more excited by the cave or by his first flashlight. Eventually, we put him on his feet and handed him the light. He switched it on, pointed it straight into his eyes, and turned away, hurt and bewildered. I still flinch to think of the pain of that disappointment.

We tease him now, but maybe the joke's on the grown-ups, because isn't this the mistake we all have made and the disappointment we all have come to, accustomed now to blinding light? Inside our houses, lamplight bounces against the windows, reflecting our own faces peering into a night we have made impenetrable. Standing on the sidewalk, we lift our faces to the stars, but the yard lights, the streetlights, the stadium lights blind us. Our security lamps create sharp and menacing shadows, making us afraid. We are caught in our own headlights. It's not that artificial light is a bad thing; it's just that we haven't learned how to use it so that it reveals more than it hides.

Our son is an ecologist now. He has learned to use a flashlight. Follow him into the dark forest, and he will show you how to hold a flashlight close to your eyes and direct its beam into trees to reveal the reflected eye-shine of spiders. He will show you where to point your headlamp into saltwater to see the yellow-gleaming eyeballs of broken-back shrimp. Follow his black light into the desert, and you can make out the glow of scorpions in the moon shadow of heaped rocks.

But sooner or later, he will ask you to turn off the light and stand for a while in darkness. That's when moonlight catches in the spines of the cholla cactus, shining like a saint. At the edge of saltwater, bioluminescent algae blink in the wakes of tiny fish, and water erupts in sparks when you toss in a stone. If you stand beside him on the beach in moist darkness, the sea will lift starlight on each wave and wash it in pools around your feet. You will wade in the night sky, and joy and gratitude will flood over you, to have been given such gifts.

OLD HYMNS OF THE NIGHT

THOMAS BECKNELL

"I hear America singing," wrote Walt Whitman in the mid-nineteenth century, "the varied carols I hear." And for another century, Americans sang on—in parlors, in parks, and in other public places. We who came of age in the era of the Vietnam War sang our protest songs and folk tunes, swaying to the lyrics of Bob Dylan and Joan Baez, enchanted by the close harmonies of Crosby, Stills, Nash, and Young. We loved to sing.

Sometime near the end of the twentieth century, America stopped singing. Perhaps it was technology's rapid progress from vinyl to CD to iPod that turned us from a nation of singers into a nation of listeners. Or, perhaps we merely became spectators, conditioned by the ubiquitous screens of our monitors and movies. Gone, now, are the advertising jingles once so familiar to American consumers—tunes that could lodge themselves in the mind with a maddening tenacity: "See the USA in your Chevrolet." And earlier: "Twice as much for a nickel, too; Pepsi-Cola's the drink for you." Marketers today seduce with the image, not with melody.

Gone, too, are the hymns. In my church, and in churches across the nation, worshippers have stopped singing hymns. We chant praises, lifting hands and voices with an exuberance unknown in the churches of my childhood. There is an energy and emotional intensity that I find infectious; so I don't propose going back to the somber meters of Isaac Watts or to the sentimental refrains of Victorian hymnody. It is difficult to enjoy those faded hymns of centuries past; yet I find myself starving for lack of what was found there.

The hymns of my childhood were clogged with cleft rocks, harvest fields, lost sheep, and bloody fountains. Not everyone liked these troublesome, coarse metaphors of the Christian faith, but their raw physicality captured me as a child. I could not sing "Leaning on the Everlasting Arms" without gazing at the mighty arms of Doris, our school cook, who lifted great pots and kneaded mountains of dough. Her cinnamon rolls were legendary. And whenever we broke into that rollicking old song "When the Roll Is Called Up Yonder," I envisioned a heaven where everyone would savor Doris's cinnamon rolls. I sang at the top of my voice, "I'll be there!"

Life, the old hymns taught me, was harsh and lonely. They called out plaintively: "Are you weary . . . ?" "Earthly friends may prove untrue," began a familiar hymn that consoled me more than once. Young and old, we sang with heads thrown back, "What a friend we have in Jesus," not needing the hymnal, for the words were worn and familiar and the melody caressing. "Thou wilt find a solace there."

I went to church with the workers of fields—farmers of corn, wheat, and soybeans in western Nebraska, roustabouts from the oilfields of Wyoming, and ranchers who drove cattle and sheep across the high plains. These were practical folks who worked from sunup to sundown. What private longing drew them back into town on a sultry Sunday evening to sing old hymns in a musty sanctuary, I'll never know. Some relished the vocal agility required by "Wonderful Grace of Jesus"; others preferred the smooth, easy modulations of "The Old Rugged Cross." And a good number of the older folk clearly yearned for Beulah Land, for the open pearly gates, for the mansion over the hilltop.

As for me, those old hymns created a world, a familiar landscape of melody and words, a spiritual and emotional topography in which I could move and rest and feel at home. And it is this solacing world for which I ache. Old hymns imagined life as a geography of oceans and tempests, shadowy vales and wandering roads in which we all were travelers, journeying toward home. I want to sing an elegy to this lost world of shadows and dark journeys.

·.·

"Now the day is over; night is drawing nigh." Throughout human history, night signaled a putting away of the tools and the toys, a time of turning inward, of retrospection, of lighting lamps, of rest, of closure, of waiting. "We grow accustomed to the dark," wrote Emily Dickinson in the bleak years of the American Civil War. But no one really needed a poet to explain the metaphor of darkness. Everyone was acquainted with the night.

> Abide with me, fast falls the eventide;
> The darkness deepens; Lord, with me abide!

Today we live in a world in which darkness does not deepen, and eventide does not fall fast. We've grown accustomed to light.

Since the end of the Second World War, when the mercury vapor lamp began to illuminate our streets and was in turn replaced by the pink orange glow of sodium vapor lamps, night has steadily retreated. The stars have fled from our cities. Where once a thousand could be seen, now barely a hundred are visible. Millions of children grow up never having seen the night sky. "With the creep of light pollution," explains astronomer Arthur Upgren, "has come a far wider, perhaps more profound, loss to the human spirit." Our earthly lights are putting out the heavenly lights. We are losing a sense of holiness and beauty and mystery.

"The star clouds in Sagittarius are a burning bush," writes astronomer Chet Raymo in his contemplative book *The Soul of the Night*. "If God's voice in the night is a scrawny cry, then I'll prick up my ears. If night's faint lights fail to knock me off my feet, then I'll sit back on a dark hillside and wait and watch. A hint here and a trait there. Listening and watching. Waiting, always waiting, for the tingle in the spine."

Old hymns of the night, sung in the night, give me that sort of tingle in the spine. "Wait and worship while the night / Sets her evening lamps alight," sung Mary Lathbury in the nineteenth century. These old hymns encouraged me to stare into the night, to be a patient watcher of the skies. "Will he find us watching," asked the blind hymn writer, Fanny J. Crosby, "with our lamps all trimmed and bright?"

Out on those great plains, we sang hymns, then went out and stood behind the church under the vast, open sky and wordlessly watched the heavens. One by one, the cars would swing away from the church, raising red, glowing clouds of dust.

The gospels tell us that the disciples sang a hymn and went out, into the night of Gethsemane, into a night of betrayal and denial and abandonment. It was midnight, I read, when Paul and Silas, jailed in Philippi, sang hymns and an earthquake shook the prison. It was midnight in Egypt when the angel of death passed over the land. The Bible stories that stirred me most took place at night: Nicodemus visited Jesus, Rahab sheltered the spies, and Ruth crawled in with Boaz, all under the cloak of night. Shepherds heard the angelic chorus, watching their flocks by night. It was night when the young boy Samuel heard God calling, when Jesus walked across the water, when Jacob wrestled with the angel, when Daniel was delivered, when Gideon put out his fleece. Night was the time of conquest and the time of consecration.

Those old hymns gave us strength to go out and face the shadows of our own lives. But night has now fled along with our hymns and taken away the wisdom and beauty and holiness of dark times. We don't sing of the night anymore. The cheerful chants of contemporary Christianity never will assure me that the stumbling night of the soul is unavoidable, that the valley of shadows and uncertain paths are natural features in the topography of faith. Old hymns of the night, sung in the night, made real to me the presence of that "kindly light" that leads me on "amid the encircling gloom."

TRESPASSING ON NIGHT

DAVID GESSNER

Several years ago my wife and I lived in a house on the edge of Cape Cod Bay. The house has long since been torn down, another mansion subsequently sprouted up, another battle lost to the whims of wealth. But what the builders weren't able to destroy is my memory of the place: the morning walks across the brief front lawn with cup of coffee in hand, the welcoming of the bank swallows back for spring, the sheer drama of the sights from my study window: white gannets diving into white embroiled surf, humpback whales breaching, a great wild bluff being lashed by winter winds. Say "Cape Cod" and most people think Kennedys and clambakes and tennis, but walk this beach in December and you will know you are in a wild place. My feelings for the house—and even more for the bluff and rocky beach below it—were only deepened by the fact that I had spent summers down the street as a kid and had known this beach as long as I had known anyone or anything.

Of course if you are reading this piece in a nature book you probably know what comes next. There are no more cabins in the woods. And there were never any Edens without serpents. These days the serpents come fast and furious, squirming over and through every beloved place. We hadn't been there a month when the old house on the hill above us, the hill overlooking bluff and sea, was ripped down and work began on the hulking hotel-sized structure that would become the largest house in Dennis, our town. For the next two years we lived not just next door to the wild ocean, but to a massive construction site. The house was bad enough, but the ripping up of the trees, the building of roads, the manicuring of once wild lawn was enough to stir something close to rage even in a calm observer. "Who does this guy think he is?" became more than a rhetorical question in our neighborhood. We learned that part of the answer was that he was someone who had made his millions selling some kind of machine to pharmaceutical companies, and had decided to use that booty to build an oversized monument to himself. With the world's resources dwindling, and that same world all but yelling that "less" is the only answer, this asshole had decided that, hell-bent, he would insist on "more."

The lights were the last straw. The good doctor—for we soon learned he had a PHD and so all began to call him the Doctor (as must have the villagers who lived near Frankenstein)—had plans to illuminate us: thirty-five various spotlights, groundlights, and pool lights. His dream was to flood the neighborhood with light, to show all what he had rendered. He began his project of illumination with a spotlight that glared up at a bedsheet-sized American flag on a fifty-foot pole, light that also shone sideways into the bedroom of his nearest neighbor on Mooncusser Lane ("Now we can read in bed without turning the lights on," the neighbor told me). When those same neighbors complained during a town meeting that they couldn't sleep, the Doctor pulled on the scoundrelly cloak of patriotism and spoke of love of country and freedom. In fact the word "freedom" came up often in those town meetings, the Doctor stressing that a person should be free to do whatever he wanted with his own property. This of course is the *yee-hah* freedom of a jet skier roaring along the shore, the loud thrills of the one destroying the peace of hundreds. In the same manner the Doctor never understood how one person's freedom can impose on the freedom of others, how by shining his light he would take away what the rest of us had come there for. If this was freedom, it felt more like tyranny.

There had been practical motives for our move to the house on the edge of the water, but one of the things that had drawn my wife and me to it was the feeling of wildness. Sometimes we all have the need for something unpredictable and untamed in this predictable, commodified world, and living on the beach gave us that. But here is what all of the new lights did to my wild neighborhood: they tamed it. They diluted the black and made what had been mysterious known. Let there be light, the Doctor said, and light there was. Next we were told he would shine his spotlights directly on the beach. Why would he do this? For the usual reasons: those of safety, convenience, and, of course, because that was what was done. He was particularly concerned with people trespassing on the land he now owned, not worried at all that his lights would trespass on the night. Of course the beach had never been completely dark: Boston was only a hundred miles away, and the industrial aureoles pulsated at various points along the hook of the coast. But that confirmed rather than contradicted something I was then learning: that with just a little space, and a little consideration, it was still possible to find patches of wildness. My wife and I would take our drinks across the lawn and down the steps to the rocks at night, listening to the ocean's gruff mantra while stars stabbed out through the black. On quiet nights we listened to the lapping and on loud nights the slamming of the waves. I would often enough stumble out to the point below the Doctor's house, and there I saw the animals that stayed hidden during the day—the deer, fox, and coyotes. Night signaled the beginning of their shift, time for the humans to check out and creatures to take over. What would the animals make of the new ill-timed daylight if the Doctor got his way?

Light pollution was just one issue, of course, and we fought the Doctor on many fronts at town hall. I remember that after one heated debate, a neighbor had reached out to shake the Doctor's hand, as if to say, "good match, no hard feelings." The Doctor turned his face away from the outstretched hand and then moved his chair away with a screech across the floor. "I just want a home for my family," he whined another time, still not comprehending how his choices affected all our families. No doubt his argument of his "right to freedom," good old American freedom, helped him at town meeting, and he won more battles than he lost. He built his house, he mowed his lawn where the coyotes had prowled, and he even shaved back the wild bluff to erect a statue of a whale (spotlighted, of course). And yes, above his home the star-spangled banner still waves, illuminated by a great circle of light.

But our fight against the lights proved worthwhile. There was a clause in a regional law about preserving the "historic, cultural, literary, and aesthetic tradition" of the area, and we used this law as our bludgeon, hitting again and again, until finally he was forced to give up some of his lights and to dim others. This wasn't a perfect solution, but better than it would have been had we not fought. Now when I visit and walk the beach at night, the doctor's entire house seems set ablaze from the inside, orange fires in every window. But no spotlights shine on the beach. At least you can still stumble down along the rocky shore below the stars, and once you are under the shadow of the bluff, the light from his house is blocked. Then you can listen to the *splosh* of waves or the *wok-poosh* of waves or maybe the roar of waves, depending on the night, and stare up at the only partly dimmed stars, and let it all work on you in a way that isn't easily put into words. True, we have been driven into a smaller corner, but at least we still have a corner. And there, trespassing on the Doctor's beach and hidden under the shade of his bluff, you can find a patch of wildness. Reduced now, true, like all our patches, but still there and still dark.

IN PRAISE OF DARKNESS

JOHN DANIEL

A few years ago I conducted an experiment in solitude, four and a half months apart from human news or company in a cabin in Oregon's Rogue River Canyon, and I thought I might become a morning writer. I had no electricity, no radio, no music. I left the radiotelephone switched off. Alone in the rhythms of natural light and dark, I thought I'd get up with the birds, as the writers I most admire have done, and have my workday finished by noon, the afternoon and evening mine to nibble like a well-earned apple.

It didn't happen. For four and a half months, mid-November through March, I grumbled out of bed most mornings no earlier than ten, grinding my coffee on the cabin deck while looking down, often, at two or three black-tailed deer, who looked up at me with what seemed reproach in their large liquid eyes. I read during the day and did some journal writing, walked, fished or hunted, and performed the regular chores of garden, woodshed, and cabin. I became fully alert about the time the owls were waking and hit my writing stride on swing shift, from supper till one or two in the morning, working at a formica table by the light of propane lamps. This is more or less my pattern at home, unless I'm pressed into a more conventional schedule by legitimate work or some other aberration. I've always been a writer who sees his reflection in the midnight window and tries to peer through that image toward something more substantial beyond.

And I've always felt a mite defensive about it, as if writing in the company of darkness were somehow sleazy, questionable at best, particularly for someone identified as a nature writer. Well, to hell with that. My experiment settled the issue. For better or for worse I'm a night writer, at home or in the woods, and during my solitude I did some wondering about why it might be that I stay up half the night with the owls and moths and my pencil.

The most obvious influence of night is to limit what we can see and do, and for me this seems to foster the kind of introspective awareness in which creative work can grow. But I found during my solitude that darkness turned me outward, too. One evening early in my sojourn, I hiked home late from the river, happily burdened with two steelhead for the barbeque. Dusk turned to dark as I climbed the trail. I had my headlamp in necklace position, ready for use, but never turned it on. The trail, though indistinct, was clear enough. Where the forest opened slightly, I noticed a faint shadow moving alongside me, cast not by moon or stars but by the residual light of the thinly overcast sky. At the unlit cabin, after using the headlamp briefly to find down booties and a beer, I reclined in the La-Z-Boy chair and enjoyed, through a large window, the luminosity of early night, now with an evening planet in the west. Tall conifers stood around the meadow like a solemn deliberative council, their lower portions blended in shadow, their points and upper reaches sharply silhouetted against the sky. Somewhere among them a screech owl gave its tremulous call.

By day I could walk among those trees and note features of bark and foliage and habit that distinguish one species from another, and those that distinguish individuals within a species. I could call them by their common names—Douglas fir, white fir, sugar pine, ponderosa pine—and by their Latin names as well. But there is a blindness in that seeing. My vision catches on the surfaces of things, gets snagged and tugged about by their multiplicity. As I watched the trees in darkness it was not distinctions I saw but their commonality, not their names I knew them by but their essential namelessness. Backed by the planet's drop of liquid light and the first few stars, they announced their membership in a wilderness vaster than daylight eyes can apprehend, a wilderness to which I too belong. I felt closer to them. They seemed to have crept nearer.

·₊˙

Though I had no human neighbors, I did see human lights at night. Satellites—an alarming number—slipped silently among the stars, and once in a while a jetliner cruised high overhead, blinking its way with a whispery rumble. On certain moonless nights I saw in the southeast above Rattlesnake Ridge, the landform that dominated my view, a diffuse radiance—the luminous effluvium of several southern Oregon towns along Interstate 5, thirty to forty miles away. Twenty years ago there would have been less of a glow; fifty years ago, there would have been none. Our age is hostile to night and to all things dark—and so, paradoxically, we make night darker. As our human lights blaze brighter and reach farther, from within their field night looks blacker, and our estrangement only grows. Who can say what we are losing? Our kind, like other Earthly creatures, was born and came of age in the rhythmic recurrence of night and moon, the specked and clouded brilliance of the Milky Way. We saw the stars and somehow came to know that we were seeing them, came to fear, to hope, to wonder. Now, in this contemporary speck of evolutionary time, we wander in our own obliterating glare, lost—happily or wretchedly, but lost—in what we have made, progressively blinded to that which made us.

And not just in cities. On farms across the Midwest and Great Plains and on ranch after ranch throughout the American West, blaring mercury vapor lamps on tall poles come on automatically at dusk and shine boldly all night. Marketed as security lights, and no doubt useful from time to time, these beacons chiefly secure residents and visitors from any possibility of experiencing true night. One of my neighbors has two, which I am frequently tempted to shoot out. Yet I hoist myself by the same petard while camping, when I build a fire and stare into its lively lightedness for hours. And what am I but a perfect likeness of modern enlightened man when I hike or ski by headlamp, peering ahead in the bondage of my narrow light beam oblivious to the rest of the cosmos, accompanied at times by annoying moths just as monomaniacally addicted to light as I am?

Once in a while during my sojourn I would wake in the middle of the night and lie in bed a while, partly saturated with dream images, partly attentive to sounds—the patter of rain, a pop from the coals in the woodstove, a twig-snap from close by in the woods. At home I would probably distract myself with reading during such an interval, or my thoughts might turn busy and fretful. I might worry about getting back to sleep. In solitude I was more content simply to be; the most I'd think about would be the book I was writing, and usually I would merely drift with the night, my being astir with a sense of significance and sufficiency in my cosmos of nighted woods and starlight, and before too long I'd fall asleep again.

I wouldn't learn until four years later that my mid-night wakenings replicated an ancient pattern. According to historian A. Roger Ekirch, pre-industrial Europeans and Americans tended to sleep in two shifts separated by an hour or more of spontaneous wakefulness. Ekirch has found references to "first sleep" (called also "dead sleep," probably reflecting the exhaustion of day laborers) in the writings of Chaucer, Plutarch, Virgil, and even as far back as Homer. The interval dividing first sleep from "second" or "morning" sleep was turned by some toward domestic attentions, in bed or out, but it seems that for many it passed in a state of mind something like what I experienced in solitude. Freed from daylight distractions, refreshed by a few hours' slumber, a man or woman could lie abed in a condition of easeful contemplation akin to meditation. Robert Louis Stevenson, who experienced the phenomenon intermittently, called it a "nightly resurrection" that freed him from the "Bastille of civilization."

Many animals sleep in multiple segments. It seems to be no anomaly but the norm of nature, and was for us until industrialization brought widespread artificial lighting. A study at the National Institute of Mental Health found that subjects deprived of (or freed from) artificial light at night developed a divided sleep pattern remarkably like that of earlier centuries. Ekirch quotes a chronobiologist as saying, "Every time we turn on a light we are inadvertently taking a drug that affects how we will sleep." It occurs to me that if I hadn't polluted my evenings in solitude with many hours of propane light, I might have reverted more completely to the segmented pattern. It may make little difference whether we sleep in a segmented or unitary pattern. But it also may be that in drenching ourselves in artificial light we have forfeited a unique way of belonging to darkness, through a fertile field of nighted consciousness that a medieval proverb characterized as the "mother of thoughts." We may have lost one means of maintaining our mental and spiritual wholeness.

Reading a biography of Emerson during my solitude, I was reminded that in the nineteenth century it was common for inexpensive portraits to be drawn as silhouettes, the subject's head shown in profile as a sharply defined solid shadow. This practice waned with the advent of photographic techniques, but not everyone saw the change as an improvement. A photo, the critics argued, showed merely a particular moment; a silhouette was a timeless outline. The very fidelity of a photograph, its lit and focused precision, was felt to obscure the greater truth of spirit, which, though not directly observable, could be suggested by the silhouette.

Henry Thoreau, that quintessential morning person, also associated darkness with spirit. He took some of his rambles at night because he found it "necessary to see objects by moonlight as well as sunlight, to get a complete notion of them." Outside at dusk, he wrote in his Journal, "I begin to distinguish myself, who I am and where. . . . I recover some sanity. The intense light of the sun unfits me for meditation, makes me wander in my thoughts." In the dewy mist of a low-lying field, he reports, "I seem to be nearer the origin of things." And later, in open moonlight: "Our spiritual side takes a more distinct form, like our shadow which we see accompanying us."

Our spiritual side is of little interest to the lifestyle and reductive ideology of materialism. Spirit, after all, is unlikely to show up at a mall or under a microscope. We believe in what we can clearly see and rap with our knuckles and measure with our keen and keener instruments. (Francis Crick once tried, unsuccessfully, to measure the weight of the human soul—perhaps the most misguided experiment ever conducted by a Nobel laureate.) Spirit means *breath,* the life that breathes in all things, and it breathes in darkness as well as in light. St. John of the Cross, imprisoned for his heresies in a Spanish jail, wrote rapturously of night as the "sweet guider" that brought him closer to his God. The English metaphysical poet

Henry Vaughan felt a similar intuition when he imagined the nature of God as "a deep but dazzling darkness":

> O for that night! where I in Him
> Might live invisible and dim!

Goethe and other German Romantics revived the expansive mystery of darkness in the head-heavy rationalism of the Enlightenment, and in America, as Thoreau was taking his moonlit walks, Walt Whitman sang of night's spirited beauties—"the mystic play of shadows twining and twisting as if they were alive"—in his long poem "Out of the Cradle Endlessly Rocking." In the twentieth century America found perhaps its greatest poet of night in Robinson Jeffers, who knew a sensuous, mysterious life abroad in the dark. "The splendor without rays," he called it, "the shining of shadow . . . Where the shore widens on the bay she opens dark wings / And the ocean accepts her glory."

In solitude I felt the presence of spirit on days when drifts and roils of mist moved slowly in the canyons of the Rogue and its tributaries. One green-fledged ridge or another would partially open to view and obscure again, open elsewhere along its length, then a different ridge would reveal a portion of itself, a ceaseless shifting of gray and green. Once I watched a great Douglas fir on a near ridge lapse repeatedly into mist and then emerge distinct again in soft gray light, the same tree each time but each time freshly born, dewy with its own creation. The landscape seemed most alive, most in its element on those days. It had a gravitas, an aura of sentience, as if I had been allowed to see into the slow, secret life it withheld on days of brighter weather. A line of Emily Dickinson's kept recurring to me: "Nature spending with herself / Sequestered Afternoon. . . ." It was the paradox of that particular country, I came to see, that it most revealed itself when partially veiled.

In the short days of winter the sun sank behind the woods to the west as early as three thirty. As the high, west-facing slope of Rattlesnake Ridge turned a deepening green-gold, a tinge of ghostliness came over my immediate surroundings of meadow and woods. The crisp shadows of afternoon dissolved, and in a progression without increments it seemed that their constituent darkness interfused the remaining light. Silence gathered with the dark, even as the river whispered a bit louder from the bottom of the canyon. Apple trees, fence posts, deer in the meadow, all singular things withdrew into background, less and less present, insubstantial as fading memories. And then, with twilight, the council of trees, magnified in silhouette, monuments of a mystery I could not speak but which the trees appeared to state quite clearly against the softly glowing sky.

．．＊

We believe too confidently in eyesight. Through most of our doings we carry around us, like a snail its shell, a room veneered with that which is visible from moment to moment, and we tend to call that paneled room reality. But even in broad daylight, eyesight shows only a pittance of what is. As I hiked or fished or sat on the cabin deck, my vision gliding or hopping between features of woods or meadow or river or ridgelines, noticing this and noticing that, the real action was in the vast sectors of the unseen—the miles of fungal filaments in any ounce or two of forest soil, the prodigious traffic of food and fluids traveling the xylem and phloem of trees, the manifold borings and diggings and chewings and excretings of countless hidden insects, the even more arcane activities of bacteria and other tribes of the very small, the groundwater seeping inches a day deep beneath me along bedrock joints and aquifers of sand and gravel, and the far slower progress of tectonic uplift raising the Klamath Mountains as the Rogue and its tributary streams cut downward . . . And those are only a few of the smaller mysteries, ones I can get my mind around. The universe, physicists are saying, seems to be mainly composed of a substance they call dark matter, invisible and so far undetectable. From the play of charmed subatomic particles to the reaches of interstellar space, Nature is largely a creature of darkness.

When I fished I couldn't see far into the sliding green current and lively riffles where I cast my line. As my lure throbbed against the current or bounced along the rocky and sandy bottom, I was feeling in the dark, trying to read braille, sometimes sensing a strike just before it occurred—the rod suddenly arched and thrumming with an unseen power thrusting this way and that, showing itself in glints and shadowed surges as I worked it nearer and finally, if I was lucky and it wasn't, raised it to the light of day where it didn't belong, a sleek iridescence flailing in my hands as I unhooked it. A few of the steelhead I caught I killed for meat, but it was the strike and play I fished for, the sudden calling of that wild energy awakening the same in me. Most of the fish went back to the river, their dark backs blending almost instantly into the opaque green depths.

Creative writing, like any art, is a kind of fishing. Poems and stories and essays arise from depths where the writer must feel for them in the dark. They rarely arise fully formed, but they never arise unformed at all. Like a fish on a line (many of them tenuously hooked), they manifest themselves in resistant glimpses—associations, bits of story, darts of feeling or idea—and the glimpses carry with them intimations of an order, an unseen wholeness they are part of. To realize that wholeness takes luck, patience, and usually a lengthy interplay between the headlamp of applied consciousness, which works the glimpses into provisional wordings, and the darkness beneath the surface—the deep river of the human psyche, fed by weathers of experience and springs of innate knowing, stirring with dreams, intuitive promptings, the murmured, insistent, half-heard urgings of spirit and soul.

An afternoon spent fishing seemed always to lead to a good night of writing, but most of my nights were good in any case. Whether I was in the cabin or out walking, the continuum of day-turning-night charged me, re-excited my interest in the work I would soon turn to with the lighting of the lamps. Little breaks outdoors—to watch Orion in the southern sky, or listen to rainfall on the covered deck, or howl into the canyon wondering if one could be conscious and truly wild as well—pepped me up as swing shift progressed and rounded the horn of midnight into graveyard. Maybe I need the company of darkness to stimulate my own darkness within, to excite its interest (or perhaps to excite my interest in it), or maybe it's just a matter of feeling at home. They are shy and tentative things, the stirrings that want life in words. You won't spot a mole in the light of sun, but at midnight, in the stillness of dark, he might just poke his nose aboveground.

Ultimately I can't know why I write at night, and I don't need to know. The things of darkness belong to darkness. As X. J. Kennedy has written in a poem, when the goose got too curious about where her golden eggs came from, her head ended up in a dark and very unfortunate place. I do know that I want the lit particularities of the observed world in my writing. I want the jags and curves and rough or silky surfaces of material things, their hues and heft, the *exactly this* that they present. They save me from the futility of vagueness. But I also want in my writing the dimness of dusk, the shadowed hiding places of daylight, the silent swirl of a deep river pool; I want misted mountains and the given light of stars and moon and the full dark of a new moon night. When I see little clear, I seem to see farther, deeper. Night saves me from the tyranny of appearances. In darkness I remember that it is not knowledge to which we most deeply belong but mystery, and I sense in the mystery of night a beauty that exceeds even the great and notable beauties of the daylit world.

DEEP IN THE HEART

SUSAN HANSON

"The stars at night are big and bright." Like most children growing up in Texas, I learned these words early on. Though I could never do the clapping part in sync with the other kids, I loved singing about a prairie sky that was high and wide, about fragrant sage in bloom, about coyotes wailing by the trail. It was a fiction that appealed to something deep in my six-year-old psyche. The fact that I'd never experienced any of it was irrelevant to me at the time.

The Texas that June Hershey depicted in the lyrics of this popular song was a Texas I knew only in my imagination. It was the black-and-white Hollywood version that I saw on Saturday afternoons, a movie set that was nothing like the green and humid landscape through which I wandered as a child. My Texas was far more claustrophobic than that, canopied as it was by live oaks and pecans, and overlaid with St. Augustine lawns and oyster shell drives. It was Horton Foote's *Trip to Bountiful,* not *Riders of the Purple Sage.*

No, what Hershey celebrated in her 1941 hit—and what Perry Como and Bing Crosby sang about in their best-selling recordings of the song—was not the reality of Texas, but the myth. In this larger-than-life Texas, the one portrayed in early westerns, anachronisms abounded. The central Texas town of Waco, for example, was sometimes depicted with mountains in the background, not Blackland Prairie. Set designers often included Joshua trees for effect, even though this plant grows only in the Mojave Desert, hundreds of miles to the west. And the iconic saguaro, a native of Arizona's Sonoran Desert, was a given; a western film simply wasn't "western" without it.

Contrived as this image would later seem, it was one that, as a child, I wanted to believe. I wanted there to be coyotes howling in the distance, not just the neighbor's dogs barking incessantly at nothing. I wanted the world to seem open and limitless, a landscape uncluttered by billboards, uncut by roads. And I wanted the sky to be dark, studded only with moon and stars.

My first inkling that I needed what the night had to give came to me on a boat ride years ago beneath the stars on Tres Palacios Bay. I was around fourteen, as I recall, and was spending the week at the Texas Baptist Encampment—the Southern Baptist way of saying "church camp." For a mere seventeen dollars I was getting an upstairs bed (and therefore a breeze) in a two-story early 1900s beach house, church twice a day (not including the morning Bible study or vespers in the amphitheater after dinner), "unmixed" swimming (separate times for boys and girls), and the opportunity to wear my circumspect turquoise "knee knockers" (something like Bermuda shorts but worse).

Most important of all, though, I was getting a chance to experience the night in a new and notable way.

The trip had begun at twilight. Our destination, appropriately enough, was Sundown Island, known locally as "Bird Island." Roughly eighteen miles from the campsite in Palacios, it sits at the intersection of the Matagorda Ship Channel and the Intracoastal Canal, more properly called the Gulf Intracoastal Waterway. To reach it, our excursion boat would cruise through Tres Palacios Bay and out into the larger Matagorda Bay. It would take us several hours.

Sundown Island, as I would later learn, is in reality a low-lying spoil bank created in 1962 from material dredged from the Gulf Intracoastal Waterway. Over the years, the Army Corps of Engineers has added fill, both to expand the island and to replace sand eroded by strong currents and the wakes of passing ships. Now a seventy-acre Audubon bird sanctuary featuring several man-made marshes, Sundown Island is covered in vegetation—huisache trees and salt cedars, sunflowers and lantana—much of it planted by volunteers. It is also an important nesting site for waterbirds, including brown pelicans and roseate spoonbills.

At the time I saw it in the mid-sixties, Sundown Island looked more like an ordinary sandbar than a sanctuary of any sort. Even then, however, visitors weren't allowed to stop and satisfy their curiosity by taking a walk on the beach, meaning that when we reached the island, we simply turned around and motored back to camp.

Some memories come to us like snapshots—precise, crisp, complete in every detail. Others are Impressionistic paintings, more concerned with capturing the mood of the moment than in rendering a realistic scene. My memory of that boat ride home is of the latter sort.

"[T]he darkness embraces everything," Rilke writes in his *Book of Hours*. "It lets me imagine / a great presence stirring beside me. / I believe in the night." For the apophatic mystics—St. John of the Cross, Teresa of Avila, Meister Eckhart—God was not to be found primarily in moments of illumination, but in what one fourteenth-century writer called the "cloud of unknowing." Rather than attempting to define God according to God's attributes—God *is* Love, God *is* Peace, God *is* Eternal—the follower of the via negativa, the apophatic way, realizes that she can never reduce God to language or concepts. Like the anonymous author of *The Cloud of Unknowing*, she contends, "He may well be loved, but not thought. By love may He be gotten and holden; but by thought never."

What matters to a person of this temperament—and I do believe that temperament has much to do with it—is the *desire* to know God, not the possession of the knowledge itself. Accustomed to paradox, the apophatic mystic encounters the divine by recognizing the impossibility of doing so; what he most longs for is also what he must be willing to give up. This individual is someone who knows the limitations of language, yet continually searches for a way to describe the ineffable, the experience of "no-words." This is the man or woman who enters a strange house in the dark, without flashlight or lamp or architectural drawings, and instead of panicking at the inability to see, feels inexplicably safe.

And safe was exactly how I felt that summer night on a boat, on a bay, in the dark.

I can't claim that I came away from camp that year with some new understanding of either myself or the world. If anything, I was about to enter one of the most turbulent times of my life. What I *can* say, however, is that through this experience, I discovered my affinity for the night.

Leaning on the rail of that boat, my legs outstretched on a

wooden bench, I considered the heavens not for what they could teach me about the positions of the stars, but for what they could show me of Mystery. It was—and is—a knowledge I now carry in my flesh, like blood, like something invisible and wild, like a pulse beating deep in my heart.

Forty years later, I live in a corridor of light that extends, almost uninterrupted, from just south of San Antonio through Waco, on to the Dallas/Fort Worth Metroplex, and north toward Minnesota. Following Interstate 35 to its end on the Canadian border, this strip marks the western edge of what might be called the "24/7 world." Look at any map that illustrates the level of light pollution in the United States and you'll see a clear line of demarcation running through the heart of the country. To the left is relative darkness, California being the main exception; to the right, a luminous web, dense almost to the point of coalescence.

When our daughter was very young, she sometimes enjoyed standing on the driveway with her father and me, naming the constellations—or at least trying to. The one feature she always identified correctly was what she called the "dip star," Polaris. Years later she would lie on the trunk of her parked car, her back against the rear window, her eyes fixed upon the night sky. Having made herself comfortable, she would stay outside for an hour, sometimes longer, just watching for shooting stars. She always saw at least one.

Today when I walk to the end of the drive and scan the heavens for familiar shapes, I am often disappointed. Where once I would have seen Ursa Major, I all too often find an empty sky, its stars erased by the glow of the nearby outlet mall. And I am not alone. According to a study published in 2001 by the Light Pollution Science and Technology Institute in Thienes, Italy, and the U.S. National Oceanic and Atmospheric Administration (NOAA), 99 percent of all people residing in the continental United States "never see a truly dark starry sky." Further, the study notes, "More than two thirds of the U.S. population, about half of the EU population and one fifth of the whole world's population live where they no longer have the possibility of seeing the Milky Way with the naked eye." That's a significant landmark to lose.

In the mythic Texas of my childhood, the stars at night were always "big and bright," and the Milky Way was a dusting of light in the southern sky. Nowadays—for those of us who live in the gravitational pull of a city such as Houston, Austin, or Lubbock—those stars glow dimly, if at all. Like the interstates that connect these urban centers, our skies tell us little about where and what we are; one place, one night is no different from the next.

The loss is more than aesthetic.

"The heavens are telling the glory of God . . . ," the psalmist writes. "Day to day pours forth speech, and night to night declares knowledge. There is no speech, nor are there words; their voice is not heard; yet their voice goes out through all the earth, and their words to the end of the world."

I long for the knowledge of night, for stars and planets, for comets trailing tails of cosmic dust. I long for words unspoken, for the inexplicable pull of so-called empty space, for the singularity that draws the soul into itself. I long for the presence of darkness.

NOCTURNES

LAURIE KUTCHINS

We harm ourselves when we diminish with our lights and busyness all that night is. I offer up some darkness knowing that night is more than an absence of sunlight, more than a horseshoe of hours bracketed by sunset and rise. I invoke night as bedrock of wound and healing, the cradle for magic, mystery, and love. I advocate and defend it.

Night is larger in its roaming than any specific time or place. But it is treated as an inferior, a lesser twin to day. We think we accomplish so much more with our eyes open. We forget how much sleep and dreamtime matter, how much our deeper seeing begins there. We neglect how much we need night's animals to go about their business in the dark, and we underguard their nocturnal domains. Evenly governed by celestial patterns, by sun and a devoted moon, we forget night is a touchstone wherein we form and fortify our most resilient selves, our souls.

Restore your eyes, rest your blinking lids. Trust the night path. Let your ears work to know this night. Listen to its maps and stories, its inexplicable music. There are so many things the darkness gives. Our vast celestial milk and shadow, our love cries, our fear and sorrow cries, the current of sperm to ovulating egg, the crashing tides of labor and birth, death and loss. Diurnal creatures anxious in dark times, don't mind that you can disappear, become lost. The night knows who you are, how to find you. Let a star or a night bird guide you.

Somewhere on this earth there is always night. A small child not yet afraid pitter-patters across a dark flooring. She is quiet and lithe as a spirit, long past midnight. She is getting her best ideas from the dark. A dream and a baby need the darkest hour to latch and nurse. A boy grows tall in his sleep. A woman and a man stay married. The old curl closer to death. Lovers love or disintegrate. Even the shadows rest. What is dangerous is how we fear and disrupt the sunless half of our orbit. We threaten so much of its work.

Say the word "Shenandoah," and you will find yourself near old Appalachian hills, looking up. Shenandoah is an Algonquian word meaning "daughter of the stars." Over us are the Pleiades, the daughters of Atlas turned into stars as protection from the pursuit of Orion. He is up there too, great night hunter with sword at his belt. And the scorpion that may have fatally wounded him also crawls the heavens. Hunter and hunted, sleepwalker and dreamer.

Let them sing and speak, oracular stars.

Even in the middle of the night in Virginia, I can smell the lamp oil we burn after dark at my family's western cabin. For much of my life I have been coming and going from a log cabin my father built on a remote piece of ridgeland bordering Wyoming. It is a modest place with massive weather and mountains, no winter access, no electricity. We've done what we can to keep it, but the surrounding valley has been besieged with growth in the years since it became my summer ground.

That the ridge made it to the millennium without electric power was no small milestone. The Rural Electric Cooperative had been trying to reach this deep into unpopulated terrain for the better part of the twentieth century. A small group of neighbors—hermits, backcountry skiers, and cabin owners—upheld a precedent set by the two brothers who homesteaded and refused to hook up way back when. Miles and Karl had kept nights dark up here, so why couldn't we? Midsummer of 2000 we gathered at the old homestead to celebrate the progress we had staved off. As dusk darkened to night and the stars began to appear, we lit candles and kerosene lamps. Our shadows flickered along the low-slung ceiling and ax-hewn logs notched into place by the brothers almost a century before.

My friend visiting from Oregon belly danced in costume to music from a battery-powered boom box. The dogs barked back at coyotes in the swale, and the children flocked in from games to be entranced by the dancer's shadows, her belly, bangles, and coiling arms. The adults passed around a bottle of silky bourbon. Here's to the homesteaders, we toasted. They didn't buy in to the grid and pressure of the modern day. Despite the new subdivisions and the valley's booming population, we'd tried to keep some homesteader spirit on this ridge. Here's to the Monarch cookstove, the root cellar, the windmill, and the homestead's two-seater outhouse, we swigged. Here's to the night, lit only by a cloth wick, a Milky Way, and a moon.

But precedents set by two homesteader ghosts and a handful of solar neighbors could not keep power off the ridge forever. New neighbors kept appearing, among them one set on all the conveniences. She organized and brought electricity to the ridge in the fall of 2005. It's fitting her name is June, the month of summer solstice, longest daylight, least night.

Because I, too, rely on electricity everywhere but at our cabin, must I dismiss its arrival there as a small, incidental shift in the big scheme of things? Night used to be a colossal darkness that lay across this western valley. From our cabin perch I used to keep my eye on three small white buttons of light in the distance. They were the rural towns, glimmering at night, diminutive and vastly separated by pasture, cropland, stream and river—whole quadrants of underdeveloped darkness between them. Upon my arrival at the cabin each June, I would stand outside toward midnight and count the same seven lightbulbs visible to me from the dark sweep of the valley's north end. These seven were barn or porch lights, a sparse and dispersed human constellation twinkling out of a hundred-mile nightscape in my view line.

Now everything spills together, nights feel dimmer, noisier. Year by year I've watched the valley floor evolve into a smear of lights and traffic. Over the moonlit slopes, the hay meadows, and wetlands along the river, nightfall now stimulates the bright confetti of stadium lights, subdivisions, and faux ranchettes. I've stopped counting the lights between my post office and my porch, and I no longer take for granted the smell of a soaked wick, the flicker of light so dim inside its glass you must curl carefully near it to read.

Each June, I will still perform my ritual cleaning of the antique oil lamps. In counterpoint to the grid, I will bring them down from storage on the top shelf, wipe them clean, shine their glass globes, trim or replace their wicks, freshen their amber oil. My children may grow to disregard my obsolescent habits, and even choose to join the grid someday, but I doubt they will ever forget those soft tongues of light upon the cabin logs during bedtime story, or its scent lingering in the dark long after.

I was always a daughter of the stars. Wyoming is among the darkest places on the earth—so much space, so few people. As a child I learned how to live with dark night in ways that were formative and generous. I grew to trust and even need its paradoxes of fear and grace, brilliance and darkness. Before I was old enough to understand, I gathered a kind of spiritual fortitude from so much undiluted night.

My father loved to camp, the more mountainous and remote the better. We slept under stars, amid the hulky shapes of sagebrush, rock outcroppings, wind-crooked pines, alpine cirques, and flowers above timberline. We zipped ourselves in while the fire was still alive with a little heat and light. Those nights taught me to trust my ears, the dark bony labyrinth of the cochlea that ever manages the night shift as we sleep. I heard the cold roar of the creek, black tongue where I squatted to wash my face. I heard the mountains chiseling their geologic puzzles. I heard the wind and ground harden with frost.

Some nights the Absaroka bears circled close enough for us to smell them. They pawed the ground for the buried spines of our pan-fried trout. The moon grazed the elk meadows, the constellations caravanned like gypsies. I slept between episodes and always seemed to wake far too alert in the icy hours before dawn, long after the heated rocks wrapped at our feet had frosted back into hard obtrusive lumps. My father snored nearby, my mother sighed in her sleep, my brother and sister lay still and unresponsive. I was boldly alive, and alone. Even the moon and stars, the bears, and sleep itself seemed to have moved on and left me stranded in a cold flannel bag in a night so black I could not see my own hands.

Survival by stealth and solitude coldly awaiting the first signs of dawn isn't so terrible. I learned to keep as part of me a girl that can outlast the night. I learned to listen. I heard the coyotes, the shriek of elk without the evidence, the wolf and the owl. Deep in the hold of night an intimacy formed between my wakefulness and my world as it neared the cusp of day. Here were night's most memorable solos, songs of sleep and prowl, a celestial stillness and silence made up of so many earthly sounds.

Some nights the night out there felt like the safer place to be than in a house or a family. It was not the night I feared. It was my parents' humanness, how they clashed in my ears. The nights my father shook the house fuming, my mother sobbed, the nights a chair or table broke, a door slammed after him as he walked out, followed by a strange calming absence in the dark, followed by my mother's hands at the piano. Debussy's "Claire de Lune," a Chopin nocturne—consolation was her playing that music by feel.

·.*

C. G. Jung, the Swiss psychiatrist and mystic, observed that we often try to displace our human shadow when we are unconscious or driven by fear of it. Until we can own our shadow, and our fear, we will project it outward and elsewhere. We try to banish the shadowy, least recognized parts of our selves. We push our difficult and darkest patterns onto literal night because we have not learned how to give them orbit within us. We try to annihilate a darkness that is essentially one of our great teachers.

Night should be a time of spiritual interrogation, a space to constellate the displaced parts of our psyches. But to know night in this intimate way we must at one time or another relinquish to being "in the dark"—our idiom for being lost, for journeying into the unknown without light switches, quick fixes, or simple consolations. St. John of the Cross called such a journey the "dark night of the soul." Like a constellation comprising many different stars, dark night is a plurality, a convergence of timing and placement, of inner and outer circumstances, loss and renewal, blindness and seeing anew. Dark Night is the soul's domain, metamorphic terrain where flashlight, grid, and maps are useless.

Soul is psyche, a star that never sleeps within us, a radiant, trusting voice-pulse that searches and sorts. Psyche needs darkness to join with love itself. In Apuleius's tale, Psyche is wedded to a mysterious husband she has never seen but comes to love in the dark. She does not know he is Eros, god of love. He comes to her only at night, forbidding her to gaze upon him. But one night Psyche lights a lamp while he sleeps, and sees he is Eros, an extraordinary loving god, not the hideous serpent of which her jealous sisters warned. A drop of hot oil from her lamp burns and wakes him. Betrayed, angry, Eros banishes Psyche from his domain.

Fear and confusion about whom to trust—her conniving sisters or a husband she knows only by voice and feel in the night—are Psyche's undoing. But her exile initiates her full powers of illumination. Psyche journeys through her Dark Night of the Soul; she searches and sorts, grieves and pleads, climbs a dangerous mountain and descends into the depths of the Underworld to regain the love of Eros. In the end, Pleasure, a daughter, is born of their dark nights.

The tale of Psyche and Eros continues to be relevant even today. We need stories that validate not only literal night but the worth of our interior darkness. We need them all the more when "power" is our word for electricity that breaks the dark, and when we assume knowledge comes fast and easy—a few seconds on high-speed Internet—rather than through the incremental soul-work of Dark Night. The human soul will always mourn the loss of eros and darkness, and should, as Psyche does, go to great lengths to restore them.

Both inner and outer night are spaces where we can meet the shadows rather than project them elsewhere, where love can come to us mysteriously as a divine presence we touch and are touched by. Bidding love and soul to bring forth pleasure from the dark, night becomes less dangerous, less endangered.

·.+*

What constellations work on us at four in the morning, the darkest hour? My daughter at the age of three does not need to know their names or their tales of trouble and flight. She needs simpler things from the night. In the dark of the cabin she's crying out. She needs something I cannot give her when a star instead of mother is the most compelling promise of her wakefulness. She needs no nightlight to soothe the transition from sleep to waking, no light switch to guide her to the night.

I am too sleepy to be a good mother. Sharply I ask what is wrong and expect her to cry out a thing she fears like "a bad dream," or "I need to go potty but I'm afraid to go to the outhouse." But she wails according to an altogether different urgency: "I want to go out and see the stars!"

"Well, go, then," I snarl down in reply. My voice stings my daughter's face. She knows I am angry being awakened for something as small as a star. She goes silent. I can barely hear her feet feeling the floor, her hands unlatch the cabin door. Silent as a drifting caddis, she floats away.

Small as she is, and groggy as I am, the magnitude of what she has just done begins to sink in. Barefoot and determined, she has just crossed an important threshold. Without mother, father, older brother, or even our dog beside her, she has gone *out there,* to find the night on her own terms. All on her own she is meeting with things nocturnal, dark and celestial. I lie still under the quilt, too sleepy to go after her, too stunned to fall back asleep.

I watched the moon set behind the mountains before I came to bed, so I know this night will be as radiant and pure as it will ever get for her. The sky over my girl will be wild and generous and uninterrupted. When she looks up, the Milky Way will be a giant spill, a long, wide band across the night startling as the white stripe down a skunk's back.

My mind begins to consider the animals that share this hour, possibly in proximity. Black bears and even grizzlies roam near enough; moose, porcupines, skunks and coyotes, great horned owls, harmless field mice . . . and the mountain lion that dens in a neighboring drainage, is he nocturnal? Like a great but dangerous secret, my knowledge of him makes me lunge from bed. What if my daughter has wandered away, like those nameless children that haunted me as a child when word of their inexplicable disappearances into nights and woods trickled down into my ears. I am bounding for the door when I hear it jiggle open. My voice gentles. "Ava, is that you? Where did you go?"

"Out to see the stars, like you said I could, Mommy." I hear no fear in her voice, only starlight and joy.

"What was it like?" I inquire of the dark as we settle back into our beds.

"It was quiet and there was a sagebrush out there that looked like a big coyote."

"You weren't afraid to be out there all by yourself?"

"No. I knew it was a bush and not a coyote."

"And the sky?" I press for more. "Did you see the stars?"

"Yes," she says. "They were all over me!"

⋅₊˙

Beneath the April zodiac of the Shenandoah I attend a Take Back the Night rally organized annually by the university students. Their mission is to raise awareness of sexual assault and violence through testimony, speakouts, and candlelit marches. It is an international initiative, going back to nineteenth-century England where women took to the streets en masse, for protection and protest against those who harassed or hurt them if they went out alone at night.

Tonight as the ground darkens under the scattered stars, the grass we've gathered on emits a pungent, lovely smell after so many months of sleep, the earth active and fertile again. I know this as the scent of Persephone returning from Hades, her abductor and husband-god of the Underworld. Her return ushers in the growing season, and the joyous evidence of a mythic mother-daughter reunion imbues our gathering. The dogwood, redbud, weeping cherry, the plum and pear all shimmer in blossom; the lilac, azalea, and peony swell in fat bud. Their flowering mingles with the strong musk of nearby fertilized cropland, intensified now by nightfall, candles lit outside, and young men and women taking back the night. I know the night is not the thing to fear. It attends its own rally. This spring night seems to participate.

Amplified by a microphone, the testimonies almost overshadow the enfolding darkness. A sophomore tells of attending last year's speakout and facing the blocked memory of her stepfather's hands at bedtime. A young man honors his mother who survived a rape before he was born; another admits he fears going out at night because he is "not your typical jock." A woman whispers of a date rape, another of a stranger in a doorway late one night.

A few weeks earlier I had met with the student coalition responsible for organizing Take Back the Night. My question was how central is the night as a presence to their mission? Was it pertinent, essential—or dispensable, merely a suggestive hook? The students were emphatic in reply, agreeing that night is a necessity, both literal and metaphoric. It is a charged and pivotal space in how their initiative informs and illuminates those who attend.

"Night is often the bad part of what happened to you," one student began, "so I think you are literally facing your fear by telling your story to the dark." Someone else spoke up: "There is so much shame," she observed. "When you can tell your story in the dark, you are more concealed, less exposed, and you actually feel safer and less ashamed speaking it into the night." Another added, "You are also saying 'I don't have to keep quiet about it.'"

As others joined in, I began to hear their voices differently than when we had begun our conversation about night and the meaning of taking it back. Zodiacal mythology instructs us that the stars were once humans, people not unlike these students, often victims of unwanted sexual pursuit, but protected, metamorphosed, and even immortalized by a compassionate god or goddess. I am comforted when I remember that people once spent so much time outside under the night sky that they found a meaningful architecture overhead. They studied and storied the same sky we still keep our rhythms under. But we shelter ourselves from night, and diminish its potencies by our frenzy for well-lit spaces, resisting what it might demand of us, or bring forth. We eclipse the important stories and maps that still abide there.

Now I listen to the students' testimonies as if the immortal voices of the stars were leaning down and speaking through them, telling their stories of rupture and recovery. These students could be descendants of the Pleiades, the seven sisters in the constellation Taurus who were spared abduction and rape by being turned to stars. "The night is the night," one is saying—"a time to be cleansed," echoes another. "What you can change is how you come to live with the night," says another from a dark place. A new voice pipes up: "The night is our chance to move through our fear, and to transform it," a truth reinforced by one who says, "We become each other's light in the dark." Another reflects, "Although we carry these wounds, we still need to trust the beauty night gives back to us."

After their voices have amplified the darkness with reckonings wise and brave and timeless, it is the night itself I come home to. Cloistered by hills, beside my dark house and shed, the night is almost complete silence and stillness but for the sounds of the spring peepers down near the creek, the call and response of two owls on Green Hill.

Why do we fear night's beauty, I wonder, and why do we violate what we fear? I think we'd do our best seeing, our deepest listening, if we could abide the dark. This, too, is testimony and witness: to go out into the night, alone and without light, to not fear the rich darkness, but to fear the loss of it, to take it back for its own sanctity. The stars of the Shenandoah are more urgent here beyond the lights of town. I follow them a long while before I go inside.

PART TWO

THE SKY, THE STARS

In this section, five writers focus on the night sky. In her "Ode to Jeff Cobb," Jan DeBlieu lies under the night sky as a way to deal with her grief. She writes, "The stars are dimming, blotted out by the lights of spreading development that seems driven by a supreme lack of vision." Astronomer Chet Raymo follows with "Why the Night Sky Is Dark," providing a history of human views of the sky and arguing, "We have squandered night with a surfeit of artificial light. We should protect the darkness that is left." While many of us take the night sky for granted, in Ken Lamberton's "Night Time" we read the story of a man who had no choice—he wasn't allowed to see the night sky. Christopher Cokinos shows in "A Backyard History of Light" how our current glut of artificial light has developed, and reflects on the wonders we can see simply by standing in our backyards. And in "Ladder to the Pleiades," Michael P. Branch learns a basic truth of stargazing from his three-year-old daughter, Hannah: "if you don't go outside and look up, you won't see anything."

ODE TO JEFF COBB

JAN DEBLIEU

My friend Jeff Cobb died last week, leaving behind a wife and two sons. I reacted as I often do to news that's unbearably sad—by going outside to look at stars.

It was ten o'clock, and Cygnus the swan was near the top of the sky. Cygnus has been described as the windshield of our solar system, because the Sun and all its planets drift in its direction under the tug of galactic gravity. When you look toward that cross of stars, you see where we are going.

I walked out to the street, a quiet dead end, and lay down on the pavement for a better view. The tops of the loblolly pines waved in a light wind. I'd studied Cygnus on dozens of nights. But it looked different from evening to evening, depending on the clarity of the sky. Tonight it seemed that a cloud of stars was visible just off the head of the cross, or the tail of the swan, depending on how I chose to see it. Through my binoculars I could make out points of light and a pebbly texture that hinted at hundreds more—the Milky Way, mostly obscured by the lights of my town.

That's where our world is headed, I thought, toward a region of scattered light ringed by darkness and confusion. I could easily believe it. The Cobbs' younger son and our son are best friends. My husband's name is Jeff, too. Like Jeff Cobb, he's a quiet southern man with a northern wife who, shall we say, doesn't need any assertiveness training. Karen and her youngest are very blond; my son and I are brunette. We used to joke about the two Jeffs with their salt-and-pepper wives and their salt-and-pepper sons. I've lost other people who were close to me, but I couldn't remember ever feeling worse.

A triangular pinch of stars, many with a bluish tint, hovered a short distance to the northeast. Beyond them Cassiopeia, the sprung W, balanced crazily on one end. Perseus was just coming into view over the trees, leaping feetfirst, leading with the famous double cluster of stars. Years ago when my household was mired in sadness, the sight of Perseus on a crisp night had cleared my senses of worry and reopened my eyes to beauty. Back then it was my Jeff who suffered from an intractable illness, a deep depression that seemed to have stolen his soul. I moved through those days and months numbly, wondering what I could do to make him heal. At night I escaped the stifling atmosphere of our house by coming outside to study the stars. Straining to see to infinity, reveling in the specks of light and surrounding darkness, I found the clarity of mind to survive.

Now here I was again, pondering the universe with a hole torn in my heart.

Auriga, the charioteer, was rising above the pines, a pentagon of stars holding some foggy patches that would reveal themselves as star clusters, if I would only look through my spotting scope. But I lay on the pavement, my hands and binoculars resting on my chest. During my husband's illness and the years following, I'd learned so much about the Universe—how it has expanded at different rates through its life, how astronomers believe its shape to be flat, how the stars are hung in a great network of arches that resembles a honeycomb. It was all so interesting! I'd learned to look beyond my own world for a beauty and intricacy that would carry me out of myself and make my problems diminish in scope, until they took on a size I could manage. I had felt supremely lucky to live in a place with skies dark enough to enjoy the stars. But then the latest real estate boom washed over my islands. In three short years ambient light erased most of the Milky Way.

Everything in this world seems to be getting worse, I thought. The country's at war. The atrocities are mounting. We're all aging; people dear to me are starting to sicken and die. The stars are dimming, blotted out by the lights of spreading development that seems driven by a supreme lack of vision.

Above me Perseus sparkled, oblivious to pain. I focused my

glasses on a small circle of stars, a shape that has always reminded me of the head of an animal, but that in fact forms the youth's thigh. What would it see, I wondered, if it were an animal looking down? A tiny woman pinned to the street, yes, but what more? Would it be able to look through me and behold my soul? We can see so little of what really matters in life. Our vision is clouded by our prejudices and misconceptions, by grief and fear and ambition. That was why I loved looking at the stars, with their pure, uncomplicated light. I had fought back against light pollution by purchasing a pair of top-quality binoculars. When I looked through their lenses, the Milky Way was mine once more. But I couldn't help wondering how much more I'd be able to see with them if the night skies were still clear. Stargazing was supposed to be a release from my usual worries. Why did the degradation of nature always seem to hit me so squarely in the face?

Perseus merely shone down at me, gorgeous but cold. Any solace I found in the sky would come from within the confines of my own imagination. The night's beauty, steeped in my own thoughts and emotions, yielded peace. But I knew I wouldn't find peace now until I could quiet my mind long enough to float free of this world. Just look, I told myself. Don't worry about anything else. Don't focus your eyes. Don't even trace the constellations. Just drift among the stars and lose, if you can, this earthly weight, all these stones of grief holding you down.

I closed my eyes for a moment, then opened them suddenly, imagining they were the aperture of a camera, set wide to take in light. I released the tension in my forehead and jaw. The cold night air stung my nostrils but seemed to open me even wider. Starlight entered me, seeping deep inside me with diamond flashes, cold whites and warmer golds, subtle blues and reds. I relaxed, feeling lit from within. I moved from point to point, feasting, taking in all I could of the night sky. We are always here, the stars seemed to be telling me. We will outlive the trials of your world. Even when you can't see us, we are waiting.

WHY THE NIGHT SKY IS DARK

CHET RAYMO

In a poem titled "He Wishes for the Cloths of Heaven," William Butler Yeats muses:

> Had I the heavens' embroidered cloths,
> Enwrought with golden and silver light,
> The blue and the dim and the dark cloths
> Of night and light and the half-light,
> I would spread the cloths under your feet.

But he is poor, the poet continues, with only his dreams. So he spreads his dreams beneath his lover's feet, gently urging, "Tread softly because you tread on my dreams." Few more beautiful words have ever been put on paper. Yet the poem never made much sense to me, for surely the one thing that belongs to all of us, rich and poor, are the cloths of heaven. Impoverished poets and billionaires have equal access to the beauty of the starry night. In fact, many of the poorer peoples of the world, in the less-developed countries, have greater access to the darkness, for they have been less able to pollute the night with artificial light. The blue-dim tapestry of night—spread from horizon to horizon, studded with diamond lights, and embroidered with the golden and silver threads of the Milky Way—has inspired religion, myth, mathematics, and science ever since the first sparks of consciousness ignited in human brains. Even today, in our technologically sophisticated times, a view of the night sky from a truly dark place cannot fail to inspire dreams of grandeur and of a meaning greater than ourselves. Yet, the dark night is endangered.

We are animals who evolved in a world without artificial light. Our brains were sculpted as much by darkness as by light. The planet turns on its axis, bearing us from the Sun's light, to half-light, to night, to half-light, and back to light—again and again. Nothing, absolutely nothing, in our ancestors' lives, not even the changing seasons, was more constant, more certain, than the diurnal immersion into darkness. Out of fear and convenience, they confined their vigorous activities to daylight hours, and spent the dark times huddled together in waking and sleeping dreams. Dreams are the fruits of darkness—exhilarating, terrifying glimpses into the labyrinthian chambers of the mind, the source of our most brilliant inspirations and deepest fears.

No wonder poets so love the dark. In the bardic schools of ancient Ireland, young poets in training were assigned a theme by their teacher, then sent to private cells furnished with nothing more than a bed upon which to lie and a peg upon which to hang a cloak, and—most importantly—without windows, not even a crack through which light might enter. There, in total darkness, the young students were expected to compose their rhymes, throughout the night and all of the next day, undistracted by a single ray of the Sun. Then, after a complete cycle of the Earth on its axis, they emerged into the light and wrote down their lines. We remember that only after the poet Dante had made his way through the Dark Wood, with Virgil as his guide, did he see—really see: *E quindi uscimmo a riveder le stelle.* "And so we came forth again and saw the stars."

Our ancestors were starwatchers perforce. At night they crept out of their caves or crude shelters, and the glittering dome of night arched from horizon to horizon, filling half of their visual field. What did they make of it, that light-flecked canopy of darkness? Today, we would say that the stars are scattered across the sky essentially at random. But our ancestors were frightened by chaos, and so they imposed familiar images upon the stars: animals and gods, agents of good and evil, tribal totems. The darkness was a screen upon which they projected their hopes and fears and dreams. The dark night was the first book of poetry and the constellations were the poems.

Throughout the night the unchanging patterns of the stars crept unhesitatingly across the sky, a hand span every hour, lifting their lights above the eastern horizon, extinguishing them in the west. In the north or south, the stars went round and round, circling a still point in the sky, the celestial pole. As the seasons passed, the patterns of stars that were visible in the evening changed: Orion and his dogs in the winter, the great birds Cygnus and Aquila in the summer. Twice each year the Milky Way swept overhead, a flowing river, a bridge between heaven and earth. Parents took their children beyond the campfire's circle of light and recited the poems of the constellations, and so the poems were passed from generation to generation, and the night became less frightening, more familiar.

·,·

"In a dark time, the eye begins to see," wrote the poet Theodore Roethke. It is one of the oldest themes of literature. Isaiah said it too: "He who walks in darkness has seen the light." Every cultural tradition has its nocturnal vigils, its dark nights of the soul. Poetry without darkness is not poetry at all. Yet we seem bent upon surrendering the darkness for a mess of electric light. As I write this, a team of men from the electric company is mounting a streetlight on the utility pole at the end of my driveway, a poorly designed light, certain to send a yellow glow up into the sky where it does no good whatsoever. Progress? Security? I ask the students in my astronomy classes: How many of you have seen the Milky Way? One student in ten raises a hand, those few who have spent some time away from cities and suburbs, in a wilderness camp perhaps, on a sailboat at sea, or in some remote holiday location. It was possibly the Milky Way's faint light, spilling across the darkness, that inspired these lines of the seventeenth-century poet Henry Vaughan:

I saw Eternity the other night,
Like a great Ring of pure and endless light,
All calm, as it was bright;
And round beneath it, Time in hours, days, years,
Driven by the spheres

Like a vast shadow moved; in which the world
And all her rain were hurled.

The dark night is one of nature's most precious gifts, a rare and valuable cloth embroidered with the history of our race, which we fritter away to our detriment.

·.*

Giordano Bruno was an almost contemporary of Henry Vaughan. Their lives might have overlapped had Bruno's life not been cut short by the Roman Inquisition. He was burned at the stake in 1600 in Rome for a long list of heresies, including the idea that the Earth, orbiting the Sun, is just one of an infinitude of inhabited worlds. The stars are other suns, he thought, receding into the distance without limit, and inhabitants of a planet of any star might foolishly think they were at the center of the universe.

Bruno was born in the Kingdom of Naples in 1548, only a few years after the death of Copernicus. At the age of twenty-four he was ordained a Dominican priest, although his curious and uninhibited mind had already attracted the disapproval of his teachers. Within a few years of ordination he was accused of heresy. The idea of heresy meant nothing to Bruno; he claimed for himself (and for others) the *libertes philosophica,* the right to philosophize, to dream, unfettered by authority or tradition. Like the poet Vaughan, he saw in the heavens a ring of pure and endless light, a universe of such infinitude as to terrify his contemporaries. Bruno embraced the infinite worlds with zeal. He was a modern in many qualities of mind: materialist, rationalist, a champion of free and skeptical inquiry. He made no distinction between matter and spirit, body and soul, and yet he was profoundly aware of the "vast shadow" that moves upon the face of the night, in which the world and all her rain are hurled.

Poet, philosopher, loose cannon: Bruno wandered across Europe all his life—Italy, Geneva, France, England, Germany—stirring up a fuss wherever he went, shaking up preconceptions, rattling complacencies, asking philosophers and shopkeepers to stop for a moment and entertain a doubt or two. The universe and God might be bigger than we think, he said. In 1591, at the request of a prospective patron, Bruno returned to Italy, to the Republic of Venice, perhaps because he was homesick, or perhaps because he sought the chair of mathematics at the University of Padua, which he knew to be open. It was a big mistake. Soon he was denounced by his erstwhile patron to the Inquisition. He was extradited to Rome, where he languished in a prison of the Holy Office for seven years, struggling to accommodate his tormentors without forsaking his principles. Accommodation proved impossible. In February of 1600 he was taken gagged to the Campo de' Fiori (Field of Flowers) and put to the stake. Years ago, on a visit to Rome, I made my way to the Campo de' Fiori, now a busy market square in the center of the city, to see the place where Bruno was burned. A melancholy and somewhat sinister statue of the philosopher stands in the square, erected by secular humanists in the nineteenth century when the unification of Italy liberated Rome from direct papal rule, a dark and brooding presence among the bustle and brilliance of the market.

Bruno was a dreamer. His vision of an infinity of worlds was a poet's dream. But within a decade of his execution the dream came closer to reality. The vacant chair of mathematics at the University of Padua was offered to Galileo Galilee of Florence. In the winter of 1610, Galileo turned the world's first astronomical telescope to the night sky and saw things that would change the world forever: the mountains of the Moon, the moons of Jupiter, the phases of Venus, spots on the Sun, and a myriad of tiny stars that twinkled beyond the limits of human vision. He communicated these extraordinary discoveries to the world in a little book called *The Starry Messenger,* in which he claimed that the universe might be infinite and contain an infinity of stars (prudently, he did not mention Bruno, although surely he knew of the radical philosopher and his fate). A copy of the book made its way to Johannes Kepler in Prague, the most important theoretical astronomer of his time. Kepler disagreed with his Italian colleague. If the universe were infinite and randomly filled with stars, he said, then the entire celestial sphere should blaze with light as brilliant as the face of the Sun. No matter which way we look into space, our line of sight must eventually terminate on a star, just as a person in a wide forest must in any direction eventually see the trunk of a tree. And since the night sky is manifestly *not* as bright as day, the universe cannot be infinite. The universe must be finite and bounded, concluded Kepler, and what we see as black night is the dark wall that encloses the universe. Kepler's argument was compelling, yet the idea of an infinite universe was in the air, and succeeding generations of astronomers struggled to explain the darkness of the night sky. One person who wrestled with the problem was the nineteenth-century German astronomer Heinrich Olbers, and the puzzle has come to be known as Olbers's Paradox: *If the universe is infinite, and contains an infinite number of stars, why is the night dark?*

Some scientists suggested that if interstellar space is not empty, gas and dust would absorb the light of distant stars. But if the absorbing matter exists, it would eventually become hot enough to re-radiate the energy it absorbs, maintaining the brightness of the sky. The discovery that stars are clumped into galaxies also failed to resolve the paradox; Kepler's argument can be applied to galaxies as well as to stars. In the end, the resolution of the paradox came from a surprising quarter: The universe had a beginning—15 billion years ago, according to the big bang theorists. Because of the finite velocity of light, as we look out into the universe we are looking backward in time. If we see a galaxy 15 billion light-years away, we see that galaxy as it existed 15 billion years ago. We cannot see galaxies more than 15 billion light-years away because there hasn't been enough time for their light to reach us. Even if the universe is infinitely big, the part of it that we can see is finite, and therefore the number of stars and galaxies we can observe is finite. This is the resolution of Olbers's Paradox: *The night is dark because the universe is young!*

What would Bruno have made of this news of the universe's beginning—the premier astronomical discovery of the twentieth century? He would certainly have applauded the questing spirit and independence of mind that led astronomers to embrace the big bang, even though such a notion violated their intuition of what the universe should be. To do philosophy, one must first put everything to doubt, said Bruno. Einstein agreed: The most important tool of the scientist is the wastebasket, he said; if the evidence of the telescope is otherwise, then his own precious theory must be modified.

Bruno might also have enjoyed the fact that the big bang is implicit in an observation that is available to everyone—philosopher and shopkeeper, poet and shepherd. We step away from the campfire, away from the ring of artificial light. Above our heads the stars are scattered like gems on a jeweler's black cloth. Standing in darkness, we are witnesses to the universe's beginning.

·,·

Once I had the pleasure of talking about the stars with a group of students under clear dark skies at the Caribbean Marine Research Center in the Bahamas. The center has an island all to itself with just a few generator-driven lights. From where we were standing, far away to the south one could just make out the faint glow of George Town on the island of Exuma, but overhead the night was jet-black and filled with stars, so many stars it was difficult to make out the patterns of the constellations. I pointed out familiar things—Orion, the Pleiades, Polaris, the bowl of the Big Dipper peeking over the horizon. I also showed the students things they had never seen before, things visible only under truly dark skies: the winter Milky Way flowing at Orion's back; the faint Beehive cluster of stars in Cancer; the Double Cluster in Perseus; and the zodiacal light, streaming vertically from the western horizon, sunlight reflected from dust in the inner solar system. Earlier that evening we had watched a thirty-hour-old Moon, startlingly thin, kiss the horizon with its eyelash arc.

These things were commonplace to our ancestors—to Bruno, Galileo, Kepler, even Olbers. Beautiful things. Hints of the majesty and complexity of the universe. As we watched from the dark

Bahamian isle, we tried to imagine ourselves whirling on our multiple journeys—on the spinning Earth, orbiting the Sun, in a spiraling galaxy, and racing outward from the big bang. We saw, or imagined that we saw, Vaughan's "Ring of pure and endless light, / All calm, as it was bright." We saw, or imagined that we saw, the spheres "in which the world / And all her rain were hurled." That's all gone now in many parts of the world.

Imagine listening to a live string quartet outdoors in Times Square at rush hour; that's the aural equivalent of looking at the night sky from the environs of a city or suburb. Go to the website of the International Dark-Sky Association (www.darksky.org) and look at satellite photographs of the nighttime Earth from space—all lit up like a Christmas tree. The northeastern United States, in particular, appears in the photographs as a sprawling luminous blotch. Europe and Japan are ablaze. All of this light directed upward has no utility on the ground; it provides no security or convenience for our nighttime activities. It does, however, scatter through the atmosphere and shroud the planet with a baleful glow that obscures the stars. Light pollution is especially troublesome for astronomers. Their ability to peer deeply into the universe is severely compromised by artificial light. The Mount Wilson telescope, which Hubble used to discover the expanding universe, now sits mostly useless on its mountain above Los Angeles, in a sea of artificial light. Increasingly, astronomers flee with their instruments to the last remaining dark sites in the world—the mountains of Chile, the high extinct volcano on the big island of Hawaii. But as the world's population grows, these places too will be impaired. A hundred years from now our major research observatories will be in space, or on the back side of the Moon.

The International Dark-Sky Association tries to educate the public on economically advantageous lighting alternatives that accomplish the required purpose—business, travel, security, aesthetics—while being minimally intrusive where light is not wanted or needed. They estimate that wasted, upward-directed light costs the United States alone a billion dollars a year. They make this analogy: If we had a water sprinkler system that wasted much of its water by scattering water everywhere—onto the street, through our neighbor's windows, and upward to encourage evaporation—we'd not tolerate it for long. If we wasted a billion dollars' worth of water this way every year, we'd declare it a national disaster. But more is at stake than money. The wasted light deprives us of something important to the human spirit—knowledge and experience of the universe that spawned us, the dark night that inspires the mystic and the poet. The students I spoke to at the Caribbean Marine Research Center were aware of the need to keep the sea and atmosphere free of chemical pollutants. However, like most of us, they had not given much thought to one of the most pernicious pollutants of all—wasted light that separates us from the majesty of night.

·.·

We live near a brilliant star, the Sun, and we experience darkness only if something blocks the Sun's light. We can of course shut ourselves up in a lightless room like the student poets of bardic Ireland, but what blocks the Sun's light most prominently is the Earth itself. As the Earth turns each twenty-four hours, it carries us again and again into the planet's shadow. We spin into our envelope of darkness—"the blue and the dim and the dark cloths / of night"—dreaming in the shadow of the Earth, glad for the light and warmth of the Sun, but grateful too for an unimpeded view of the deep universe. We have squandered night with a surfeit of artificial light. We should protect the darkness that is left. To those fellows from the electric company putting up a new streetlight at the end of my drive, I say, "Tread softly because you tread on my dreams."

NIGHT TIME

KEN LAMBERTON

The first night after I got out of prison, I realized I had become afraid of the dark. I was lying in bed and my wife turned out the lights. I thought I had gone blind, as if a simple flip of a switch had severed my optic nerves. I closed my eyes, then opened them. Closed them, opened them. No difference. I couldn't even feel my eyelids moving—and that's when the fear came, rushing over my body as if an unexpected rogue breaker had caught me dozing on some winter beach.

I couldn't remember a darkness like this, not in twelve years.

⋅⋆⁺

At Echo Unit, walking the chain-link perimeter was one freedom permitted us, and I circled the half-mile exercise track every evening "listening for the eruptions of grace into one's life," as Kathleen Norris says. On those nights, after the sun slipped beneath the grenadine rim of the earth and the Santa Rita Mountains looked like cutouts pinned to my southern horizon, I was graced by a sky unfenced. Bright Venus dangled beneath the moon's eggshell. Jupiter shone like a fleck of mica in the southwest. Orion, my winter indicator, mounted the eastern sky. I felt their pull in the liquid of my cells, where they competed with other gravities for attention. The sun, the moon, the earth, that place—I tried to fathom the geometry of it all, settling the lights in their orbital planes. Planets, stars, constellations, the blackness of space. It was the one direction out of the place that had no edges—light years of unobstructed line-of-sight. Ageless photons for my finite retinas. "But if a man would be alone, let him look at the stars." I, like Emerson, used to stare at the night sky and feel my own insignificance. But in prison, where I was hardly even a number, the stars made me feel differently. They helped me to understand that I was part of a greater thing, not the greater thing itself. And it didn't escape my notice that the brightest lights—the moon and planets—owed their brilliance not to their own internal fires but to their ability to reflect light from a greater source beyond themselves.

·‚*

In a place where the only privacy allowed came beneath the sheets, I cherished the darkness. What there was of it. Floodlights on the perimeter fence and on high poles across the prison yard created a hazy smog of light pollution so dense that nighthawks seined it for food. The foraging birds flashed like beacons as they dipped in and out of the cones of light, feeding on a plankton of insects. The lights snapped on with an electric whine as dusk settled upon our cordoned backlot of desert south of Tucson.

And even in our housing units we had no escape from the security of light. "Lights out" meant some lights went out while others came on. Extinguishing the light in my cell only allowed the bright hallway outside my windowed door to lay a column of chalky alabaster across my face. Blocking the window risked a disciplinary write-up. Covering my face invited a rude wake-up. Too many times the rapping of a flashlight on glass disturbed my sleep as some guard on graveyard shift attempted to get me to show some skin so he knew I was real and not a stuffed blanket.

But occasionally, the glory of darkness overshadowed me.

One night, a guard roused me at 3:30 AM, asking me if I smelled smoke. Then he ordered me to leave the building, and I followed a crowd of men outside. It was cold in my T-shirt, but the unexpected absence of security lights treated me to some gorgeous constellations. Ursa Major stood on its tail in the north: Alkaid, Mizar, Alithoe, Megrez, Phachid, Merak, and Dubhe—I could still name the Great Bear's seven major stars, stars I had memorized to impress the woman I would marry. (While holding Karen in my arms under a Tyrian hemisphere of summer night, I would whisper those stars into her hair as though I was quoting poetry.) Leo, also rising on its haunches, dominated the southeastern sky with Regulus. High in the southwest and only 8.8 light-years distant, Sirius was planet-bright. And nearby, I could see Orion for the first time that season. The star-girded hunter was my favorite constellation. The red giant Betelgeuse on his right shoulder is four hundred times the diameter of our own sun and 270 light-years away. Blue Rigel at his left knee is twenty times the diameter of the sun and 650 light-years away. But I saw the supergiants in the constellation as if closely connected with lines drawn in the sky. To see Orion is to look hundreds of years into the past, and more, to beginnings—not of time but of the stars themselves. The seeds of stars germinate in the nebulae of Orion's loins.

When a meteor laid a neon track across the blackness, I remembered the Leonid meteor shower. I concentrated my viewing toward Leo, the constellation from which the meteors seemingly originate, and they came. For forty-five minutes, while the inmate fire-response team geared up and dragged hoses into our housing unit, I watched the sparks fall. Some left brilliant blue green trails in their wake that held for seconds and then faded. The men around me saw them too. I heard their pleasure every time a particularly magnificent rock splashed into the atmosphere.

The fire turned out to be only smoke from a burned-out heating unit, and the guards too soon herded us back into the glare of our cells. There, I closed my eyes to darken my mind and remember the sky.

·,·

On some evenings, when a scarp of purple nightfall rimmed the horizon beneath pure, dustless, indigo skies, the desert amplified the stars. If I could find a dark corner away from the intersecting penumbrae of the security lights, I could lie on my back and listen to them.

At these times, I looked to the stars for confirmation that I wasn't stuck in one place. From one hour to the next I could mark the counterclockwise motion of Ursa Major and know that the earth moved beneath me. I was spinning with it at 700 miles an hour. From one season to the next, I could feel the earth coursing against a backdrop of constellations, summer's Scorpio and winter's Orion. I was circling the sun at 66,000 miles an hour, a million and a half miles a day. I was not in prison. I was a traveler. A galactic tourist, visiting the sun and moon and gas giants. I watched the universe pass by from the broad window of this fenced plot of ground. I should have had motion sickness.

·₊˙

Before I went to prison, I believed that my connection with the moon and stars kept me from being afraid. I could pass whole nights alone in the desert because they gave me direction and a way to light my way. How could I get lost when Polaris always stood brightly in the north? When the moon cast both light and shadow onto my trail?

Prison threatened to break my connection with the night sky. To replace the night with halogen glare, which gave only blinding, disorienting light. Under prison's scrutiny, I felt exposed, humiliated, abandoned to the consequences of my crime. Prison rubbed my face in what I had done. Prison said I was unredeemable. Prison couldn't show me any future because it always pointed to my past. And, although I couldn't always see clearly in any direction, I believed in the possibility of moving forward. "The future is dark," Rebecca Solnit says in *Hope in the Dark,* "with a darkness as much of the womb as of the grave."

·₊˙

The worst threat came the day of my transfer from Tucson's Echo Unit to a lockdown facility at Yuma, Arizona, the result of some distant faceless administrator's notion to punish me further. As if *being* in prison wasn't already punishment enough. I had arrived at Echo Unit only two months previously, after working nine years toward gaining a minimum-custody status and placement there. I *wanted* Echo, to be near Karen and our three daughters, to feel the "freedom" of a prison where I didn't have to spend twenty-three hours a day locked inside a cell.

Echo was an "open" yard, a minimum-custody prison and part of the Tucson complex, a square-mile prison city that comprised six other units of higher-custody levels where Arizona incarcerated forty-five hundred men and women. At Echo, four hundred and fifty or so men lived in housing units and dormitories, recycled trailers used during construction of the Alaska pipeline. A library, education center, chapel, and dining area dominated the center of the yard. Men played basketball on painted courts and volleyball and softball on green fields. Echo was a place of grass and trees and sidewalks lined with rose bushes. An exercise track traced its perimeter. There, on summer evenings, teenage boys strummed guitars under leafy cottonwoods while old men sat on park benches with doves on their shoulders. I thought of Echo more as a monastery than a prison, although I was certainly no monk.

The transfer began in the predawn darkness as officers woke dozens of us from sleep, rolled up our property, and locked us into leg shackles and belly chains. Then we boarded white, unmarked school buses and left Tucson. All I could think about as I stared through a heavily screened window at the receding mountains was how far away Yuma was from Karen and the girls. Four hours' distance might as well have been three years' separation.

We headed west on Interstate 8, passing volcanic plains, creosote flats, and sand. More and more sand. The Yuma prison complex, I learned, wrestled with encroaching sand dunes three miles from the U.S.-Mexico border.

I was part of the last wave to arrive at the Cheyenne Unit, a medium-custody, controlled-movement yard. Officers removed our shackles and packed us into chain-link holding cages. We paced the eight-by-twelve cages for hours, waiting for housing assignments. After dark, the temperature began to drop. What was taking so long?

We were anxious and uncomfortable. I still hadn't shaken the irrational feeling from the afternoon that we were being bused into the sand dunes for execution. When several men suddenly jumped up and scattered away from one side of my cage, the largest scorpion I'd ever seen—longer than my boot—crawled under the chain link. *Welcome to Yuma prison.*

Then something happened on the north yard. Officers appeared from the administration building and ran across the tarmac, their radios squealing. Within minutes, the officers had two men in custody. A bloody bandage covered the side of one's face. Another man they locked into the last empty cage, leaving his hands cuffed behind his back. He watched us for a while in the shadowed glare and then said, "You won't make it on this yard."

I didn't last twenty-four hours at Cheyenne. Inmate threats against me led to staff threats. Officers told me, "If you won't give up names of who's threatening you, we'll send you back to the dorm and you can deal with it." I refused to comply, and I had company. Men from Echo had already been hurt. Lawyers were making queries in response to inmates' phone calls. I had also managed to make a quick call home, and I took comfort in imagining Karen erupting like a solar flare, burning prison officials to ash with her words. Dozens of inmates from Echo "volunteered" for "investigative lockdown" at Yuma's Central Detention Unit (it's like going to jail in jail) rather than stay on a prison yard with a population of abusive inmates.

I joined three other men from Echo in a concrete prefab cell, where we had to ask an occasional guard to remotely flush our toilet. We bathed in yellow hospital glow; at Yuma, even darkness was contraband. I passed the time with my face pressed to a narrow window, my eyes pulling darkness through the slot of thick glass. My horizon was undefined except by a receding tide of sand, and I began to believe that the sand and the sky could trade places without notice.

Two weeks later, I was the only inmate to return to Echo Unit. Few men in prison have advocates like Karen. On that first October evening, I walked the edges of that marginal place and rejoiced. To see the constellations again, Cassiopeia and Cygnus, to watch nighthawks flutter like great white moths, to smell redemption in the gloaming dust—I felt as though I had been released from prison.

·,*

At Echo, to see a world in a raven's feather holding night against its vane was an excess. To see a universe in the rising moon as pale as a communion wafer was an extravagance. There's something to be said about the ability to recognize this. There are some who never see, who've been camped too long not inside prison but inside themselves. Prison can be a means or an end. It is a place where the severity that is outward might force you to look inward, and once there find another kind of darkness. Many, however, will never see this place through so much security glare. For them, prison exerts a constant presence, shouldering its way into the mind with every wake-up to the exclusion of other thoughts, particularly those concerning *why* one is in prison in the first place. Blame lashes outward instead of inward. Time does you instead of you doing time.

Ecologists say that life is the most abundant and adaptable at the margins. If this is true, then prison must be primordial soup: a place where something new could evolve out of the muck. The worst kind of punishment is that which locks a man into a cell that shuts out even visiting cockroaches. Prison needs to have margins, impermeable barriers between the caged and uncaged, yes; but also *permeable* barriers that leak if only with wind and rain, insects and birds. Prison must have margins where daylight gives way to darkness, where one can be just free enough to look up and see the stars.

I write these words, more than five years after my release from prison, on the one-thousandth anniversary of the brightest star ever witnessed in recorded history. In May of 1006, people from all over the world saw their southern sky blaze with a light equal to the moon, visible even in daylight. Today, remnants of the supernova still ripple through the constellation Lupus as a nebula rich in familiar elements like calcium, iron, carbon, and oxygen. The stuff of bone and blood, and bars.

When I got out of prison, I was afraid of the dark. But I know now that this was not a darkness so much on the outside as it was a darkness within me. Probably, this is a healthy fear, a trembling that comes from knowing oneself as a tidal eddy of stellar elements, and understanding what horror and what grace those elements are capable of.

A BACKYARD HISTORY OF LIGHT

CHRISTOPHER COKINOS

Sometime this week you were outside at night. You saw stars or you did not.

Likely you did not see 2,700 of them.

Under a clear sky free of light pollution, you could.

In most cities, you're lucky to see a handful of stars, trapped in orange haze like birds caught in oil.

·.*

Rushlight.

Candles of tallow, those of beeswax.

Lamps of paraffin and kerosene.

Streetlamps of whale oil, then of gas. Factories that could make and make and make twenty-four hours a day lit by lamps burning gas from coal. Lamplighters who moved up and down cobblestone streets with poles that torched lights against the dark: little vindications of Prometheus in London, Berlin, New York.

Eventually, Edison. Electricity. Mercury vapor. Sodium vapor. Metal halide. Cities and towns bejeweled with streetlights.

Who was the first to see lamplight from an airplane? Who could not have been dazzled, night-flying over such sparkle?

Though, over the farms and small towns, before the poles and lines that progress gave them—stars. Even their names are lovely: Tarazed, Porrima, Albireo, Polaris, Cor Caroli.

Now such inanities as the brilliant beacon of the Luxor in Las Vegas, which, like a long arm and fist, punches a hole in the dark and reams the sky with 40 billion candles' worth of light.

No one should begrudge light that falls on streets, parking lots, and entryways, light cast down so we can safely see where to go.

But even from my backyard I see a "light dome" that smears the southwest horizon over, of all places, the bustling megalopolis of Hyrum, Utah. It is summer. Kids are playing baseball at night. The light thrown up is the color of pale salmon. And to the north, not the Luxor, but lights for the twin towers of Logan's Mormon Temple, along with those for the usual assortment of big-box stores, car dealerships, fast-food joints, a university campus, and flagpoles.

Once light clarified, protected—think of Pleistocene fire-light—but now it smudges, it obscures: light like amber soot instead.

Beyond the treetops . . . stars.
White fires, scar-white, white splinters
in the palm of night. They heave and spin
toward the western edge, toward the city haze.

—KIMBERLY JOHNSON

The city haze to the southwest and the north, along with a streetlamp and a neighbor's new, oft-lit house, diminish "my" sky here in semi-rural northern Utah.

I can, however, put my house between me and much of this domesticated blaze. I face the east and southeast, where the Bear River Range rises, whose only lights are the occasional lightning-sparked wildfires among cheatgrass, sage, and juniper. Over these mountains, over Blacksmith Fork Canyon, the sky remains blissfully dark.

I count, as they say, my lucky stars. Tarazed, Porrima, Albireo, Polaris, Cor Caroli. Massive balls of gas and fusion. Pinhead streams of photons, particles nearly as old as the universe itself, having formed all of 10^{-34} seconds after the Big Bang.

About one million years later, the universe grew thin enough for sight, though there were no stars and, had there been, there were no eyes with which to see them. The first stars were born about 299 million years later.

Many billions of years after the Big Bang, our solar system formed. Dated from the present, the sun was born about 4 or 5 billion years ago.

Then, sometime in the Precambrian, eyespots and eyeballs developed. There was life that could see.

On cloudless Holocene nights, during any season, I'm often outside, looking at the stars.

In winter, I see what many mistake for the Little Dipper: the Pleiades, a cluster of young blue stars, only 50 million years old—younger than mountain ranges, younger than the ancestors of sandhill cranes. The Seven Sisters of myth. I count five, six, seven stars. More. Sometimes I break into double digits. The Pleiades test both visual acuity and night-sky darkness. In the eyepiece of my ten-inch Dobsonian telescope, I see a few swimming in a scrim of nebulosity, a hot blue fog of gas. In winter, I see the daub beneath Orion's Belt, his sword, which, in the telescope, transmutes to a wide green bat wing—the Orion Nebula, fifteen hundred light-years away. In the Pleiades cluster, stars have just been born. In the Orion Nebula, stars are being born. This is creation.

In spring, I ponder the seeming blankness of the sky, so few stars. Here the spring sky is not so much diminished by the smirk and smudge of our lights as it is by sheer distance. In spring, from where I stand—beside this hummock of Russian sage or that hedge of chokecherry—I am looking outside our galaxy. I am looking into intergalactic space. Hence, fewer stars. But what appears empty swarms with galaxies: the "Black Eye," the "Sombrero," and the "Leo Triplet."

Equally poetic to even a casual stargazer like myself are their designations in the catalogs of deep-sky objects: M64, M104, M65, M66, NGC3628. Billions of stars in a single galaxy. Billions of galaxies in the known universe. It's hard for me not to believe life exists in such vast space, as I pause at the scope from staring at a faint green blob— M100, say, one blossom from the Virgo Realm of Galaxies—to run my hands through sage, lift them to inhale the scent.

If I stay up long enough on a spring night, the stars of a summer's midevening rise. The motions of the planet and the sky bring to me the band of the Milky Way. When I stare into it, near a grouping of stars informally known as the Teapot, I'm looking straight into the center of our own galaxy. I can't see what lurks there—no one can—but I know that a massive black hole rips light from the gas and stars falling toward it. Such unfathomable violence on a peaceful, cool summer's night in the mountains. I hear the riffle of the Blacksmith Fork River, a dark thread of sound beneath starry streams of light. Canyon winds ruffle the leaves of willow and box elder. Mallards gab in the eddies. Before too long, the Teapot moves into the Hyrum light dome, and that part of the Milky Way is amputated. I am, I know, a rare soul these days: someone who can see even part of the Milky Way from his home.

In autumn, I watch for another galaxy: Andromeda, which, at 2.5 million light-years away, is the farthest object we can see with the naked eye. (That presupposes a sky dark enough for the feeble gleam to show.) For now, I see it each autumn, tangled in the dying cottonwoods where winter's eagles will perch. Andromeda to the naked eye is a mere puff of light, like a cloud. Andromeda was, in fact, for a long time thought to be a nebula, a region of gas, within our home galaxy. (The word *nebula* comes from the Latin for "vapor" or "mist.") In the telescope, however, Andromeda is so huge and so bright, no eyepiece I own can contain it. From its bright core, two tapers of light outstretch. Andromeda looks like an eye or a flying saucer.

Though stargazing has become a major industry—enough to

support two national glossy magazines and three major telescope makers—this activity is far more than a hobby.

It is a deep reckoning with the instantaneously ancient. It is a way to love nature and the seasons. We no longer plant according to cycles of starlight, but we can let such light take root in our hurried souls and grow slow peace.

·.*

I admit, though, that for all my disdain for manufactured light, I still have a childhood love for the way leafy trees look when lit by a streetlamp stuck in among branches. Such trees look like big green brains with a synapse frozen in firing. These green-bright trees are painterly and make me think of Hopper and Burchfield. They seem inherently nostalgic, at least when they're not glaring at me while I try to pick out a new globular cluster or nebula.

Now, though, I mostly mutter when I see streetlamps whose light is not cast downward, where it belongs. I curse when I see security lights mounted so they shine horizontally, temporarily blinding drivers along a road; electric candlelight burning in every window of a neighbor's house, in some homage to the kitsch-light of Thomas Kinkade paintings; or the porch light left on after a visitor has departed.

I think of the effects our lights—especially when concentrated in cities—can have on birds. According to the Fatal Light Awareness Program, "up to 100 million birds die in collisions each year." This phenomenon is not yet much studied, but FLAP estimates that "across North America, more birds die from collisions [with buildings at night and during the day] than succumbed to the Exxon Valdez oil spill." Strong light traps birds, especially during migration, and they are loathe to leave such alluring beams. Eventually, the birds die of exhaustion or predation.

Light-trapped birds may be more of a problem in large urban areas than here in the Cache Valley, but the lights keep coming. I worry about the birds and about the loss of connection and magic that comes with blotting out the stars. I worry about the new commercial business district my town of Nibley has approved, as well as the houses that are slated to be built across the river from my partner and me.

In his history *At Day's Close: Night in Times Past*, A. Roger Ekirch notes a few reasons why some individuals and cities opposed street lighting in the nineteenth century. Pope Gregory XVI thought street lighting would help the masses "foment rebellion," Ekirch writes. The city of Cologne considered streetlamps unnatural, for God had meant night to be dark. On the other hand, Ekirch also reminds us that Thomas Edison thought electrical light at night would improve us morally.

Both the pope and Mr. Edison were wrong. Not surprisingly, I am pretty sympathetic to the city fathers of Cologne. So I do quiet things: I give a developer and his family a gift subscription to *Night Sky* magazine. I hopefully send a copy of another town's dark-sky ordinance to a member of my local planning-and-zoning board. Lately I've been thinking of hosting a star party for my neighbors on Hollow Road. The last time we all got together—that is, non-Mormons with Mormons—was to sandbag during an April flood.

·.·*

So much light at night is our restlessness made visible, like Oregon Trail ruts that tourists can see in parts of the prairie and the West, except that light pollution is ubiquitous, not scenic.

Dissatisfied with the day, still bouncing hither and yon to find Zion or gold or a job with health insurance (the latter understandable to me in ways the former are not), we make the night a temporary frontier every twelve hours or so. Such a frontier needs to be as safe as possible. But it need not be so, well, so *bright*.

Like a lawn of Kentucky bluegrass in the desert, careless light is a false security and it is a waste. In more ways than one, light pollution is our failure to see.

LADDER TO THE PLEIADES

MICHAEL P. BRANCH

My daughter, Hannah Virginia, who recently turned three years old, is teaching me about the stars. Far from being a liability to her, my own profound astronomical ignorance has turned out to be her boon and, through her, a boon to me as well. The most important thing the kid has taught me about the stars is the brilliant, open secret that if you don't go outside and look up, you won't see anything. Every night before bedtime she takes my hand and insists that I get my bedraggled ass up and take her outside to look at the stars. If this sounds easy, ask yourself if you can match her record of going out *every single night* to observe the sky—something she has done without fail for more than a year now. Calculate, for example, your own ratio of commuting to stargazing, or TV watching to stargazing. It seems to me that Hannah has accomplished something impressive: she has perfect attendance at the one-room schoolhouse of night. That she has somehow brought her celestially illiterate father along is more amazing still.

Following the inexorable logic that makes a kid's universe so astonishing, Hannah insists on looking for stars no matter the weather. At first I attempted the rational, grown-up answer: "It just isn't clear enough to see anything tonight, honey." But her response, which is always the same, is so emphatic and ingenuous that it is irresistible: "Dad, we can always *check*." And so we check. And it is when we check that the rewards of lifting my head up and out of another long day come into focus. One cold and windy night we stepped out and discovered, through a momentary break in an impossibly thick mat of clouds, a stunning view of Sirius blazing low in the southeast. Another evening we stood in an unusual late winter fog and saw nothing—but then we heard the courtship hooting of a nearby great horned owl, followed immediately by the distant yelping of coyotes up in the hills. At Hannah's insistence we even stand out in snowstorms to stargaze, and while we've never seen any stars on those white nights, we've seen and felt and smelled the crisp shimmering that arrives only on the wings of a big January storm. Snow or no snow, she knows those stars are up there, and so she does easily what is somehow difficult for many of us grown-ups: she looks for them. And whether she sees stars or not, in seeking them every evening she has forged an unbreakable relation with the world-within-a-world that is night.

Questions are the waypoints along which Hannah's orbit around things can be plotted, and she has asked so many questions about stars for so many nights in a row that at last I've been compelled to learn enough to answer some of them. In doing so I've stumbled into placing myself, my family, my home, on the cosmic map whose points of reference wheel across the sky. We've learned a surprising number of stars and constellations together, and we each have our favorites. Now that we're in our second year of performing this unfailing nightly ritual, we're also having the gratifying experience of seeing our favorite summer stars, long gone in the high-desert winter, come round again on the year's towering, dark clock of night.

The other evening after supper my wife, Eryn, asked Hannah to make a wish. Without hesitating she replied, "I wish I could have a ladder tall enough to reach the stars." As usual, I didn't know what to say. I long since became too grizzled to flash on sappy-ass-isms of the Maya Angelou Hallmark card variety, but it is impossible to dismiss a three-year-old kid—who, among other things, discovered the cosmos without much help from me—when she articulates hopes that are at once so perfectly reasonable and so beautifully impossible. Before she goes to sleep, Hannah and I look at the six-dollar cardboard starwheel I bought to help us identify constellations. Too tired to make much of it, I toss the disc down on her bed in mild frustration. She picks it up, holds it upright in front of her in both hands, stares earnestly out beyond the walls of her room, and begins to turn it left and right as if it were a steering wheel. "Where you going?" I ask. "Pleiades," she says. "You want to come?"

·₊*

Despite its faintness relative to many other celestial objects, Pleiades—which she still pronounces Tweety-Bird style, *Pwee-a-deez*—is Hannah's favorite thing in the sky. If you're in the northern hemisphere, this lovely cluster is relatively easy to locate: when looking south, it appears above and to the right of Orion, the hunter, the three bright stars of whose belt align to form an unmistakable fieldmark. To the naked eye, Pleiades resembles the dipper shape that is better known in the northern sky, where the big and little dippers of Ursa Major and Ursa Minor, the two bears, revolve endlessly around the axle of Polaris, the North Star. Known to myth as the Seven Sisters and to science as Messier Object 45 (M45), Pleiades is an "open cluster" of stars—not a random constellation but a close grouping of intimately related stars that were born together from a single nebula cradled in the arms of a spiral galaxy.

I still don't know why Hannah loves the Pleiades so much, and I wonder if I ever will. She gives different answers on different nights, and though she's patient with me, mostly she seems to think I'm asking the wrong question. What fascinates me most about Pleiades is not any arcana of astrogeekery, but rather the simple fact that they are beautiful yet barely visible. The nine brightest stars in the cluster all have magnitudes hovering just around the limit of sharp human vision under excellent viewing conditions. But how many you actually see depends not only upon your eyesight and the weather and the position and phase of the moon, but also upon altitude, humidity, dust, pollution, and the critical factor: light levels in the night sky. "Let there be light" may have sounded good at first, but for there to be Pleiadean light there must first be earthly darkness. Although the dimmest of the major Pleiades stars is forty times brighter than our own sun would appear at a similar distance (the brightest, Alcyone, is one thousand times brighter than our sun), only six stars are usually visible to the unaided eye. However, many people can see the seventh sister as well, and under perfect viewing conditions it is possible to see nine stars. In 1579, before the invention of the telescope, the astronomer Michael Maestlin accurately drew the positions of eleven of the cluster's stars. In Egyptian tombs archaeologists have found, buried along with mummies, early calendars ornamented with a dozen Pleiades stars, and aboriginal cultures in remote desert regions of Australia produced art depicting thirteen Pleiades. There is even some evidence that in the rarefied air of the high Andes some sharp-sighted Incan people may once have been able to see fourteen member stars. It was common among Native American peoples in North America—as it was among stargazers in ancient Greece—to measure the acuity of one's vision by the number of Pleiades stars they could see. Simply by being there, Pleiades tests the limits of our vision. These stars are easy to find, but also easy to lose. Like most things that are precious, they are there but barely, and how well we see them—or if we see them at all—matters enormously.

·.·˙

In Greek mythology the Pleiades are the celebrated "Seven Sisters," celestial daughters of the sea nymph Pleione and the Titan Atlas, whose punishment from Zeus—to bear the weight of the heavens upon his shoulders—makes my twelve hours of desk jockeying look easy. The Seven Sisters—Alcyone, Sterope, Celaeno, Electra, Maia, Merope, and Taygete—were nymphs in the train of Artemis, and I owe them a deep debt of gratitude because they served as nursemaids to baby Bacchus, the feisty little god of booze. And the Pleiades sisters must have been easy on the eyes, as many well-heeled Olympian gods, including Poseidon, Ares, and even Zeus himself, had affairs with ladies from this fine gaggle of astral hussies. Only Merope, whose name means "mortal," did not put out for the gods, a mistake for which she took considerable grief. Or perhaps the problem was that the mortal she chose to marry, that old coyote Sisyphus, was a fast-talking con man whose infamous boulder-rolling punishment made Atlas's bad day at the office seem like a moonlight stroll.

So while Daddy Atlas was too busy holding up the cosmos to stand on his crooked porch with the twelve-gauge, Orion the great hunter saw the Pleiades gals and decided to follow a new quarry. This turned out to be a bigger challenge than Orion expected, and after seven years of chasing the sisters he still hadn't scored—something that apparently drives hunters crazy. In some mythological genealogies Atlas and Orion are related, which suggests that Orion wasn't above cruising for chicks at the family reunion (in most old European languages, the Pleiades were indeed called "the chicks"). Picture the look of anger and frustration on Atlas's face while he watches all this: "Don't make me set the heavens down and kick your hunter ass from here to the underworld!" At last tired of fielding complaints from the harried maidens and their kin, Zeus gave in and performed an Olympian feat of astromorphosis: he turned the seven sisters into doves and placed them in the sky, where they had good reason to suppose they would be free from sexual harassment. So much for that: later, when Orion was killed, Zeus placed him in the heavens just east of the sisters, where he might pursue them across the wheeling night for all eternity.

"Pleiades," a Greek name lovely to both eye and ear, has a mysterious etymology. A likely origin is *plein,* which means "to sail." Scientifically speaking, because Pleiades is a cluster, its member stars do sail across the wine-dark ocean of space together, as the unrelated stars of most constellations and asterisms do not. The more direct connotation of sailing, though, is hinted at by the ancient Greek nickname for the Pleiades: "sailor's stars." The cluster's conjunction with the sun in spring and opposition with the sun in fall marked the opening and closing of the safe season for sailing in the ancient Mediterranean world. Around 700 BC the Greek poet Hesiod included this lyrical admonition in his *Works and Days:* "And if longing seizes you for sailing the stormy seas, / when the Pleiades flee mighty Orion / and plunge into the misty deep / and all the gusty winds are raging, / then do not keep your ship on the wine-dark sea / but, as I bid you, remember to work the land." Hesiod knew the winds of trade and adventure that drove Greek ships, but he also knew that to sail after the heliacal setting of Pleiades was to risk a long visit to Poseidon's coral caves. Our limits are written in the stars, he seems to say: know the time to plough the earth and not the waves, planting spring's hope in soil and not upon the furrows of the deep.

But "Pleiades" may instead be derived from *pleos,* meaning "full," which perhaps alludes to the wind-filled sails of Aegean summer but suggests other meanings as well. And the plural of *pleos* means "many," an apt description of the cluster's stars. Or perhaps the name is derived matriarchally, from Pleione, the mythological sea nymph who is mother to the Seven Sisters, and whose own name means "to increase in numbers." But the etymology most consistent with the mythic astromorphosis of the sisters is *peleiades,* which means "flock of doves." Although some believe this derivation to be merely poetic, having perhaps originated with the ancient Greek poet Pindar, many etymologists maintain that the literal meaning of "Pleiades" is "constellation of the doves." "Pleiades" stands as a lovely marker to a lost trail—a lyrical name that to this day remains unmoored and sailing.

I tell Hannah the story of the seven dove sisters, and she performs morphoses of her own, changing them into the ravens and owls and meadowlarks who are her neighbors—and back into girls, and then into stars once more. The magic of transformation is closer to her reality than mine, a fact made plain by her fluidity in imagining and describing transformations of all kinds—in herself, in her non-human neighbors, in the night sky. On the mountain behind our house, she tells me, the antelope we see so often drink together at the same springs with a local dinosaur she has imagined and named "Braucus." She's perfectly certain that pronghorn and plesiosaurs sleep in the same caves, have breakfast together, even go to the same birthday parties wearing homemade garlands of lupine and sidalcea and balsamroot flowers. The walls of the world—the ones that delineate the boxes within boxes where most of us live and work—are invisible to her. For Hannah, the net of relations that makes the universe cohere is as interstitial as it is connective: strong and flexible, but full of inviting passages between worlds, and permeable in ways that have long since been lost to me.

I tell Hannah about the science of the Pleiades as well as their mythology, but to her these two modes of perception offer equally compelling explanations for something that she experiences in a relatively unmediated way. Orbital gravity, escape velocity, open cluster, reflection nebulae—that story is fine with her. Seven sisters who, while their daddy tries to hold up the world, become doves in the night sky—that makes perfect sense too. Hannah loves stories, but behind the stories she sees only the world, just as it is, entirely full of possibility, every night when the light of the sun goes out.

· ⁺ *

Many ancient Greek temples, including the celebrated Parthenon, were precisely constructed so as to align with the heliacal rising or setting of the Pleiades. By orienting their temples in this way the Greeks were also orienting themselves within the universe—a universe in which this tiny, dipper-shaped net of stars formed a hub. The Seven Sisters are vitally important to ancient Greek culture—they figure in the *Iliad*, the *Odyssey*, and other foundational Greek texts—and their beauty is also sung by the Romans, including Cicero, Ovid, Varro, Pliny, and Virgil. But the delicate beauty of the cluster, its visibility from both hemispheres, and its importance in marking the seasons of navigation and agriculture have given it prominence in cosmologies and agricultural calendars from around the planet.

In many ancient cultures the Pleiades was considered the axis mundi—the navel or pivot of the universe, around which all else revolves. In ancient Arabic cultures the cluster was known as "Al Na'ir" (the bright one), and in ancient Egypt the ritual of the dead included speaking the names of the seven "Hathors"—the Pleiades—to assist the dead on their journey to the distant stars. In Hindu mythology the Pleiades stars were collectively called the "Krittika" (Sanskrit for "the cutters"), the seven daughters of Brahma who married the Seven Rishis, or Seven Sages. The skilled sailors of ancient Polynesia celebrated these "high born" stars as crucial navigational guides whose arrival initiated their New Year. The Chaldeans called the cluster "Chimah," meaning "hinge," because it was thought to be the point upon which the universe pivots. In China the cluster of "Blossom Stars" was recorded in a 2357 BC reference that may be the first in astronomical literature. The indigenous Ainu people of Japan saw not a blossom but a great tortoise that they called "Subaru," a name we still see on the six-star logo of the automotive conglomerate that took its name from the Pleiades. To the Maori of New Zealand the Pleiades are Matariki, the beloved "little eyes of heaven." And among the aboriginal peoples of Australia, who believe the Seven Sisters came to earth from the celestial sphere during the ancient Dreamtime, each tribe calls the cluster by its own name: to the Kulin people the Pleiades were Karagurk; to the Adnyamathanha, Magara; to the Bundjalung, Meamai; and to the Walmadjeri, Gungaguranggara.

I can also tell Hannah stories that are closer to home, since most of the indigenous peoples of North America had rich cultural connections to the Pleiades. Hannah's favorite of these many wonderful stories, which is shared by the Kiowa, Arapaho, Crow, Cheyenne, and Sioux peoples, closely links the Pleiades to Devils Tower (Mato Tepee), a sacred site that functions as an axis mundi in Native American cosmography: seven Indian girls who were fleeing a great bear climbed to the top of the volcanic tower and prayed to the Great Spirit for help, after which the tower soared upward until the girls were delivered into the heavens for their protection.

The Pleiades were also used to calibrate many ancient agricultural and sacred calendars, and festivals devised to honor the Seven Sisters have survived even into our own day. Because the heliacal rising of the Pleiades in spring coincides with the life-giving season of new growth, many ancient traditions associate the cluster with fertility and plenitude. But the cycles of the Pleiades have also marked the end of seasons, and the end of life itself. In old Europe the cluster was powerfully associated with mourning because its acronychal rising (rising in the east just as the sun sets in the west) occurred on the cross-quarter day between the autumnal equinox and the winter solstice, and thus marked All Hallow's Eve, the Feast of the Dead that was later Christianized as All Saints' Day and eventually secularized as Halloween. Traced back far enough, Halloween leads to the ancient Celtic feast of Samhain, which was calibrated to the culmination of the Pleiades at midnight. Indeed, the two prominent cross-quarter times in the old Dorian calendar were both marked by the Pleiades, and evolved into May Day and Halloween, those important pagan celebrations of life and death. The Pleiades are thus an illuminated bridge between us and our ancestors. When little Hannah dons her Halloween costume and completes her metamorphosis from girl into butterfly, she is actually participating in an ancient ritual of death and rebirth that has for millennia been marked by the movement of her favorite stars.

Given that astral worship was one of the forms of pagan idolatry against which the ancient Hebrews defined their faith, it is fascinating that the Old Testament—a book not rich in stars—contains explicit references to the Pleiades. Both are in the book of Job, and both are reassertions of God's authority as supreme creator of heaven and earth. Job's problem is that, like Hannah, he asks a lot of questions. In Job 38:31–33, the Old Testament God—who is master of, among other things, the rhetorical question—asks Job the sort of question one had better answer correctly:

> Can you bind the chains of the Pleiades,
> Or loose the cords of Orion?
> Can you lead forth a constellation in its season,
> And guide the Bear with her satellites?
> Do you know the ordinances of the heavens,
> Or fix their rule over the earth?

The correct answer, of course, is "no way, boss." Job's inability to govern the stars defines the limit of his mortal gifts, for only omniscient

God can penetrate the nebular veil that shrouds the Seven Sisters. Like Job, Hannah and I must get along as best we can, asking much but knowing little.

·.·

Among the innumerable myths about the Pleiades are many that attempt to account for the "Lost Pleiad"—that missing seventh sister we so seldom see when gazing skyward at night. Some say that Merope, having married the mortal Sisyphus, went dim with shame. Others claim that it is Electra, who in mourning hid her bright face in grief upon the death of her son, Dardanus. Scientists tend to identify the missing Pleiad as Celaeno because it is the dimmest of the seven stars and just at the limit of human vision. But even here there is uncertainty, for the fluctuations in apparent magnitude that occur over time in these stars may mean that the ancients saw a brighter seventh sister than we see today. I do not know which Pleiad is the lost sister. In one story I often tell Hannah, she herself is the seventh sister, now invisible in the sky because she descended to earth to be part of our family. She likes that story, and whenever I tell it she smiles and sings a memorable line of incisive verse: "Twinkle, twinkle, little star, how I wonder what you are."

The myth of the lost Pleiad has more serious implications in our own day, for now all seven sisters are in danger of becoming lost. Because the Pleiades stars are barely visible, even moderate levels of human-generated light in the night sky wash them away as if they never existed. Insofar as our visceral experience of them is concerned, these stars are critically endangered. If the light of the Pleiadean doves is extinguished, it will not be the same kind of extinction suffered by the passenger pigeon and the Carolina parakeet—but it will be extinction nonetheless. When I crest the last valley ridge before entering the city, I see in the southern sky the shining stars of Orion's Belt. But above and to the right of the hunter I see nothing—the sisters are lost in the hazy glow of city lights, and where there should be beauty there is instead a hole in the sky. I know that beyond the cloud of light generated by the Wal-Mart and its satellites floats a delicate net of exquisite stars that have played a vital role in human culture for millennia, but this abstract knowledge cannot substitute for the experience of seeing the sisters for myself. As Ralph Waldo Emerson wrote in *Nature,* "If the stars should appear one night in a thousand years, how would men believe and adore; and preserve for many generations the remembrance?"

When the pagans celebrated feasts to honor the Pleiades, they first extinguished every fire in the land so as to better view the Seven Sisters ignited in the heavens. Our age, too, must find some ritual to honor the stars, for darkness is the only mother from which star-light can be born. Modern connotations of the word "benighted" are strictly pejorative: "to be unenlightened; involved in intellectual or moral darkness." But the word's archaic meaning tells a differ-ent story: "to be overtaken or affected by the darkness of the night." We cannot be enlightened without first becoming benighted. What new myth can inspire us to protect the darkness that is now hidden beyond the bright map of America?

I wonder how long Hannah will continue to check nightly for the Pleiades if the light spewing from the growing city sends the other six stars into exile with their lost sister. I wonder how to measure what is lost when something that connects us so richly to the uni-verse simply ceases to be part of our sensory experience—when the nebulous glow of this celebrated cluster recedes, leaving only a blank spot on my daughter's treasure map of night. I wonder if there will be a way to know how the woman Hannah becomes will have been blessed by the presence of her sisterly stars, or impoverished by their silent vanishing into the artificially illuminated night.

PART THREE

IMAGINATION AND STORY

For centuries, dark nights inspired humans to tell stories that helped explain the mysteries of the world. In this section, five writers speak to the value of darkness as a continuing source of stories that help us understand and live our lives. In "The Month of Mornings," Alison Hawthorne Deming promises to "get out into the night, to sit and watch and listen and record," reflecting on what darkness has to teach us about the value of paying attention, of being present and alert. Ray Gonzalez's prose poem/essay, "The Desert Night," confounds our expectations and complicates our notions of chronological and traditional direction—a lot like real darkness can. Old ways of living with darkness is Philip Hiscock's subject in "Night Folklore in Newfoundland and Labrador." While these remote Canadian provinces offer cultures that until only recently lived with dark nights, versions of Hiscock's examples could probably have come from any location before artificial light. Poet Shaun T. Griffin writes in "The Seven Stories of Night" of watching the sky with his sons, and through these three sets of eyes the reader sees night anew. And in "Nocturne with Moths," Robert Michael Pyle shares fiction in which threats to the real world's "sweet darkness" and the creatures to which it is home are clearly defined.

THE MONTH OF MORNINGS

ALISON HAWTHORNE DEMING

1

The moon hangs a notch off full, hovering over the clerestory of my house, cold light at 6:00 AM casting shadows on the ground, lacy mesquite, spindly paloverde—pencil shavings on the sketchpad of desert ground. In the dark before first light, cars wind through gears as they leave the neighborhood. The rooster is up. One loud dog. One soft dog. Daylight begins as white seepage behind Agua Caliente Hill, its southeastern slope overlapping with the northeastern slope of the Rincons, this corner into which the city has crept across the basin and stopped when it met the mountain range. Smell of horses, hum of swimming pool filters. Big Dipper upside down and spilling, empty now, the floating icon that's the easiest map for reading the night sky. A sheep bleating. A musky vegetable smell. I might have drowned in the turbulence of the everyday, except for this sanctuary on the page. "To evoke night and day," wrote Robert Duncan, "is to evoke our powerful longing to fall back into periodic structure, into the inertia of uncomplicated matter." This is my promise: to get out into the night, to sit and watch and listen and record one month of dawns. The hour before dawn is the time for contemplatives. No less true here in the secular suburbs than in the sanctuaries of the religious. Neighbor's headlights spill into my space: he's going to work his bird dogs in the Patagonia hills. Rooster crows at one-minute intervals—pitch rising this time—otherwise the same note—no, there it is again—the higher note, a strained call as if insisting: Don't you get it? Pay attention! It's morning! Now a third rooster calls—throaty, deep, flat. Gray sky, white spillage of light, shadows gone. Horses banging on the metal rails of their corral. My breath passing in a gust of steam. Roosters quiet—they've done their job of bringing alive another day. The songbirds start just as a hint of pink lines the hill's shoulder. All the complicated singers wake up—wingsonged twitter, thrasher whistle, dove coo, owl hoot, and the crackle of the cactus wren—all in perfect tune. It has to be like birdsong, says Saul Bellow, otherwise why bother? Father Earth lying on his side, back turned to the city.

5

Moon in half. Bright crepuscular light. What if I didn't write? No things but in the telling. Refuse the gift and you lose that sliver of the sublime. No telling but in things. A diesel engine starts. No minister on his way to work this Sunday dawn. Perhaps a hunter. A man going to woods to work his dogs on pheasants. A woman trailering her horse to ride the mountain pass. Roosters to the east and south, voices bantering, through the space that separates them, testing with their voices to be sure they have enough space. That's me, foolish lover of the gift, who rises cold each day to do the exercise of being present by making myself absent from the house and all its excuses—like Plath's cake baking—the thousand ways that art's denial can keep a woman from the truth: that she is made to heed the halftone light and leave the calculated recipes behind. Horseshit is the loudest smell in this neighborhood. This morning it's heavy and fresh. Horses make the sweetest-smelling shit on earth, shapely nuggets breaking into gold that makes the roses bloom. Singers trill from hackberry, chainlink cholla, and mesquite. I am sitting in a bowl filled with song. A single flier—swallowlike—cuts across the blank to get from tree to tree. Pale blue the starless sky, horizon pink 180 degrees; birdsong loud 360. Another flier, smaller than my hand—a verdin?—darts, then one whisks over my left shoulder, comes back again to see what kind of thing I am that sits and sits and doesn't leave. Birds can't see at night. Except the owls. Birds can't turn their eyes in their sockets. That's why they tip their heads to see. Full light and I no longer feel the place is mine. Time for heat and tea and talk inside the house.

8

Why is the moon—three-eighths of it alight, the inner edge fuzzy—why is it beside my right shoulder when at this hour one week ago it was behind my head, sailing over the house? The moon is traveling too, as is the wind on its way to the next tree, as are the cars on their way down Mount Lemmon. Only the mountains are still, though this is true only in the lens of human time. Mountains are always rising or falling, slipping or tilting, though so slowly we see only the effects and not the process: the house settling off-kilter, stress cracks widening above windows and doors, the latch no longer catching on the garden gate. "Quartz is the frostwork of a longer night," wrote Emerson. The mountain prepares its illusion of permanence each day. "The mountains," said my mother, born in 1910 in New York City and resettling in the desert after a lifetime in the northeast, "are a comforting presence"—she who is closer to death than she can say. I drove her from the city up into the ponderosa forest and above. The mountain road was blocked by a slide, so we parked at the roadblock and stood at an overlook to take in the enormity of the land, and she gasped for breath as one does when beauty shakes the body out of habit. Gertrude Stein, tuned to the beyond, wrote, "I am not I when I see." The wind is trapped here again in this corner room of the desert, this house made of dawn, though it is warmer than yesterday and there are no clouds.

10

Sliver of moon heading east toward the Rincons. Calm, mild, winter weather, mesquite's black trunk, sculptural against the night's backlighting. Where could I go to be free from the sound of cars? A small freedom to be sure when yesterday Essie Mae Washington-Williams, the unacknowledged seventy-eight-year-old daughter of a black teenage maid and the pious segregationist Senator Strom Thurmond, announced her lineage to the world with no anger, perfect dignity. And that was her freedom—to forgive the flaws of the father. As a child

I used anger to create a safe place for myself—racing to my room, slamming the door loud and hard to be alone with emotional confusion, the paralyzing intensity of my childhood. I've spent six decades learning I don't need any longer to slam the door. Though such intensities can still possess me. Coyote raises his voice. The backup warning of a truck beeps and beeps. A motorcycle roars. The soft mechanical roar of cars is the city's pulse, movement keeps it alive, and I am part of its organism sitting in the dark, watching night give up its hold on the land, watching day slide in, this narrow band of time when both are present. The great horned owl lands in the mesquite tree beside me, flaps from one limb to another. A strong old mesquite. Its claim on the land precedes mine. Precedes the whole neighborhood and most of the city. And the owl? Five million years of hunting in the desert in the night. I turn the page. He doesn't budge. Has he been watching me for a week? I move and lean to see his shape outlined by the sky. He doesn't budge. We sit together. He turns his back to me. He looks like a cat—tufts pointing up like triangular ears. He is bigger than a cat. He watches toward the southeast where pink sunglow is rising. He is perched twenty feet from my side. He leans, he hunches his back and rises up from the branch and flies to the neighbor's slump block wall. There too he sits and watches until the thrasher's two-tone song says it's time to go. The owl's body so light and silent as it lofts from perch to perch to sky on air-filled wings.

11

An airplane comes out of the night, red and green lights blinking for port and starboard, white floods for landing. At first the flying luminosity looks like Venus, a light so bright it blocks out directional colors. At first it's silent, then passes with a murmur—tons of metal, wire, and human hope gliding above the desert. I woke up wondering what attention has to do with art. Is it enough to perceive and record and follow the spontaneous dictates of form? I hear the owl but he does not show himself this steely morning with burnished clouds hardening the edge of day. The owl is moving through the neighborhood or else there is more than one owl, soft whooshing calls rising from roosts to the south and west. A single high-pitched coyote hoots to the north coming closer—and to the east nothing but the shine of the day spilling through the mountain gap. Attention calls me from sleeping in a warm bed to being present for the moment when metallic clouds turn salmon red. Attention wants to hold the moment still, as if beauty is the prize for living, and maybe it is. My breath spills in a messy smudge of steam that melts away with the heat of my body—no match for the morning's cold. So here I sit, a bundle of cells making warmth and words and paying attention to birdsong—wren, thrasher, and Gila woodpecker. Here I am, unsure of why I do this or what it is I do except keep faithful to a form—morning exercise to bring some order to my mind.

15

Warm rain—the air cottony with mist, horses nuzzling rubber feed buckets. I've been trying to picture the moon's orbit in relation to where I sit—waiting for it to emerge from the phase called new during which it's invisible. For two weeks I tracked it passing from west by south to east—each dawn hanging at the same—what's the word—declination?—in the sky—30 degrees, perhaps 40 above the horizon. It is hard to see motion on this scale—just as hard as seeing coyote, coati, fox, or bobcat pass twenty feet beside me in the night. It is the orbit I'm watching—the monthly cycle—but how is my relation to the moon affected by Earth's spinning on its tipsy axis? There—along the edge of the scrub where yesterday the coyote lingered to smell me, something approaches, it sits. I feel the presence—but I do not see it, that animal of the night I feel watching. Was that a tail, long and sinuous, that startled from the flick of the neighbor's light, the creasing of my poly rain gear? Still. Still. It passes without showing itself. Perhaps a flicker from the cloud that hovers from receding storm. Perhaps the flicker of mind that's deeper than one lifetime remembering what stalks and feeds and preens—the animal of mind. I'm dressed for rain. The rain has passed. Yesterday I forgot to wear my glasses on the morning watch and the sky looked clear. Today I have my glasses on and the scene is milky vague. Rods, the cells that see in black and white, are sensitive to the night. The cones that see in color are better for diurnal life, but without correction, the world's a haze to me. The night may be one thing I can see more clearly as I age. Oh the gentleness of a breeze in the desert moistened by last night's rain. How many days have the coyotes passed and watched me? Are they like the doves and hummingbirds and cactus wrens who know me not by name or scent or usefulness or danger but as one of the rhythms, both regular and stochastic, that punctuates their day?

21

I wait in the darkness for something to happen—expecting the something to be new—not rooster call, cars on Snyder Road, pink and gray smudge in the sky, moonless dome of sky, under which I sit like a specimen under a lid. We invented God to feel that some entity exists that studies us, loves us—one way we name our need for love. Maybe all creatures feel as if some force can apprehend them and in that apprehension feel something like what we call love. Take the coyotes that travel alert and fast, so light on their paws, and lope along the backside of the houses wailing out their lament and song as they sniff their way through the night. God's dog, the ancients called them, because their movements carried grace and could not be controlled. How hungry I have been to lose myself in alertness to what surrounds me. Why not sleep near the man I love, wake up together, sip tea in bed, read about the origins of art, and talk? I'm not trying to accomplish something here—only to experiment with the tools at hand. I've been driven since I was born to take up in earnest my apprenticeship to life.

Glasses on. Glasses off. It's too early for my brain to make sense of the altered vision of these manufactured lenses. They're called progressives because the viewing fields are blended, no demarcation between the reading and the distance corrections. It seems I'm useless to such distinctions in the dusky smudge of dawn. One thing I can see is that the foothills mansion has finally taken down its casino Christmas lights. The house now bears a couple of outdoor spotlights, making it look to scale—that is, diminutive against the dark lavender mass of the mountain range standing dignified above it waiting for its early dose of spilling light. The perfect poem would have an infinitely small vocabulary. Is is. Tree is. Horse lips wicker softly, and the thrushes, larks, wrens, cardinals, and Gila woodpeckers, invisible but loud, rise as if from invisible vents in the ground. They all carry on like mechanical toys, God's little pets who can't get over the excitement that another dawn has broken the seal of night, the day day day day day, they all sing in complicated code, and then they try out wings and fling themselves across the sky. The syrinx is the vocal organ of birds. It uses all the air that passes through the trachea (the human larynx uses only about 2 percent of the air that passes through it). The syrinx straddles two separate tracheal tubes so birds like thrushes can make two sounds at once or take a breath without breaking the rhythm of a song. Chipping sparrow has only one song. Brown thrasher has thousands. How many dialects inhabit this song neighborhood?

26

The anomaly. The thread in the weave that's left flawed. The place where the evil can escape. Evil spirit of excessive order, control, believing intentions can determine outcomes. The place where the imperfect belongs. The day has started, morning light is not process now but fact. I lie in bed, cat at my side begging for the hand. My mother sleeps down the hall, as is her custom to sleep until midmorning. I spent the night thrashing, dry mouthed, feeling my love's embracing arm as a weight I could not bear. I dreamed there was a problem area in my tooth—number thirty-one—that showed up on X-rays. The dentist had lied to me when he said it looked fine. I saw the problem circled in my medical chart on three separate pages. Yesterday my mother experienced another TIA—transient ischemic anomaly—what once might have been called "a spell." She became tired, dizzy, afraid while we were shopping at the Goodwill Superstore. She sat down, then said the room was blurry. We sat. The room was very blurry, she said, and she could not see it clearly. She kept looking out from her body as if from a foreign place she did not understand. Then she faded—sitting with hands limp, head slumped forward, eyes half closed, saliva running down her lower lip. I put my arm around her and asked if she could hear me—no response—no recognition—she sat removed from herself, as if life had left her, though she never fell, never lost involuntary controls. A woman came to us—said lay her on her side. Yes, said the Goodwill woman, lay her on her side. And the 911 dispatcher said lay her on her side if she begins to drool. Then she began to return—a feeble yes when I asked could she hear me—vomiting—asking for Kleenex—leaning on her side with me holding her head in my hands as a pillow. A strangely intimate moment with a woman who keeps her distance. The hospital chart, at the end of hours of being ignored in the high-tech sterility of the ER, read "near syncopal event." I felt the awful disconnect between seeing my mother disappear before my eyes and the tepid words that meant "no problem." All night my head spun with the nearness of death. I kept myself in half-light all night. And now morning is half gone, the cat sleeps by my side, hot tea is waiting, the Japanese black pine newly planted beside the asparagus bed is waiting, and morning is still going on.

27

A faint light near the summit of the Rincons like a landlocked star—someone must be camping there in the cold, warming to a campfire or a gas lamp's glow as the pinpricks in the skin of the night close off and morning brings on the day's disguise—hidden, all the vastness and exploding luminosities in which our little satellite wobbles and spins around its sun, this trick of light and eyes that gives us blue to live beneath—the blue surround. Why is the sky blue? Because we live in the waking dream of perception—a honeybee sees something different with its complex eye—fractals?—does it even have a brain? Sometimes I feel inert struggling to stay abreast of the social pace—daily news, weekly work, random appointments, mess on the desk. Some days I don't even know how to have a conversation with the man I love. I long for solitude, even if only for these monastic minutes when the cold air washes my face, the backyard light next door flips on, the sky blues as the night peels back, and I fall into sync with the elements of the scene out here where the trees are making the oxygen I breathe. I breathe until I get cold and lonely and have to face my brokenness again.

THE DESERT NIGHT

RAY GONZALEZ

The desert night lizard and the desert night snake, not the rattler, but the night snake that is always there, as if the space inside the heart was blackened with time and experience. It is dotted with stars only seen at night distance, pinpointed away from city lights that blind memory before the lights go out and I finally see that each form of darkness places great distances between the past and the present moment of blindness. I find the night stars assembling as if a strange God has given me another chance to understand how the galaxy above the landscape of home is merely the back of his hand, a wrist action sending a shooting star from southeast to northwest, its brief arrow pointing to the fingers that fall beyond those black peaks and disappear. Standing in the desert night near Kilbourne Hole, New Mexico, there is no horizon, only the deep hole of earth shock, the volcanic formations below starting their sleep as the vast sky turns black. It does not move into a deep purple or blue, but a black that smothers thoughts of the past and signals it is time for the true world to emerge because the man standing on the edge of the ancient, extinct volcano has no idea about what is going to come out. The growing shadows consume the miles of thorny mesquite, cover the creosote bushes in a blinking of my eyes, the sudden drop of light weaving a curtain of fear and doubt about coming here to stand before a hole in the earth, wanting to find the source of its sinking scar, the scramble of black and red lava frozen in the second it takes to go from dusk to the blanket of night that filters thought upon thought, slowing things down in the caution of yucca plants that surround the invisible crater.

·.·

A man speaks in the place of stones, his arms burning night candles from the march toward home. He is talking and his hands reach out, bells ringing in things he does not say, unable to spell what he wants, an onion he owns rolling across the table as if a planet shrunk and he could see its white ball moving beyond what he will never know. He secures the avenues from a certain wildness, says his glass eye guarded him when he was a child, saved his angels from extinction when the eye fell out one day, rolled away like the onion now tottering on the edge of the table, its axis spinning like a blind man falling because wings are not companions, only the roads to the dusty midnight floor. Suddenly, I look up and huge barrel cacti are growing everywhere, sprouting like fat green bombs about to entomb the world. I do not know how to stop their growth around me. I bow my head, the swarming thorns pinning me to the ground, away from the fire I never saw, only felt at my back each night I tried to sleep on the bare desert floor.

I look across the crater as night falls and realize I will see only what the sky wants me to witness, and it is a complicated thing because I came here to find night shadows from my first visit to Kilbourne Hole, some twenty-seven years earlier when I was twenty-five and thought the black desert held the secrets to composition and creativity, the key to old speech and languages that would take me into the age of poetic imagination. I gaze across the approaching shadows and do not recognize them because I am much older and it has not taken that long to drive here from El Paso, but my hometown is gone as much as my sight has vanished because the pitch-black night suddenly covers everything around me and I am tempted to get in my car and pull on the headlights. I do not do it because I do not want to join what might be revealed in their illumination. I want to stand here and look up at the desert night and be unable to count the stars that move farther away, their immense white dots spinning in formations I can't name, can't sound, or begin to describe because scientists theorize that lava flowing from nearby Aden Crater spilled over the earth's surface and cooked the wet limestone beneath me millions of years ago. After a time, there was a steam explosion that produced Kilbourne Hole, which stretches for almost two miles across and reaches a depth of nearly three hundred feet in places. It is early night and I cannot fall in. I must stand here because the shadows of youth never return when I visit the home desert. Those shapes and night patterns are gone forever. As I gaze across the desert, I recompose fear as strength, as a view that allows me temporary sight from blindness to be able to witness the night releasing a setting sun, then waiting for a light that has nothing to do with volcanic dwelling, the petrified ashes of the past sinking slowly as black time goes.

Last night, I thought I heard a distant train and listened, wondering how often I had avoided crossing the tracks, the night telling me

I must have been asleep. The whistle sounded far away and made me sad with the darkness of my father, the loneliness of my mother, the ghost that appeared as my grandmother who told me, without speaking, that the train was moving across the desert where her body lay. Last night, I turned and stared at the window from the bed and heard the train crossing Paisano Street, weaving under Mount Cristo Rey, extending like iron smoke that won't blow away, the clacking of wheels bringing me unexpected joy before whispers announce I will never reach the train. Last night kept me from praying for what wasn't there, the diminishing whistle a guessing game, my lone chance gone after almost finding it after hours, the whispers of old women surprising me above the silence of the quiet night train.

·₊˙

Flying through the night in another part of the country, wild was where I wanted in—geese honking overhead, vanishing in an argument of light where doubt punishes me because I can't see. It is too dark. When I said it was the desert, it was actually the road where colored lights take over and lead me into a safer sleep. Wild was not a word at the start—a shapeless form of darkness where the hawk circled, then saturated my eyes with classical light. Nothing changed but the air where I stood, the night map guiding my imagination into tomorrow's hands, the storm upon the ridge of yucca where a cold fire waited for me to rub its ashes on the rocks, leaving a message that this is the savage order of nature I was taught about by a hidden voice, the black circle in the ground an open eye mute men leave behind in the middle of the night.

·₊˙

I want to leave the cut in the earth behind because I can't see or find my way down the cliffs and don't want to fall into the interior, can't imagine rolling down dunes of ash to finally complete the voyage—misguided step leading me down to explore what it truly means to be aware of the desert night and its power that has followed my back for thirty years of absence from the Chihuahua Desert that hides and appears, hides and appears, again, without its night resolving there is a union of light and darkness we cannot participate in as long as we walk the welcoming landscape of a home that refuses to leave us alone.

·,*

The night's eye in the foliage of famine. The bristling coyote in the tattered cottonwoods. The graves of children burned in a fire. The change of advisors leading their souls astray.

·,*

The closeness of a triangle and a tooth. The system of corn plants vanishing again, their blind roots transforming rage. The sessions from another era changing the landscape.

·,*

The imitation of arrow and sharp spleen. The coat and hat left behind the adobe wall. The pebbles by the river useless and untouched. The notes of skeletal history collected to please. The night's eye in the dance of mushrooms. The speaking owl hidden in the hands. The water moving around the green logs. The stolen glance shaping all things. The flame growing on a knot in the tree. The cluster of bathed demons breathing in balance. The sudden door closed and locked. The flimsiest of reasons saving the neighborhood in the dark. The clouds moving into the distant valley at night. The phrase lying in doubt before rapture arrives. The gate to the bridge falling into the river. The game room simply a family album. The night's eye blinking for the last time. The music from the lower spheres heard too soon. The prelude about the night the moon fell.

·,*

The desert night involves knowing how to extract wisdom from action, how to move my body across the chasm and be able to get home with my eyes opened and closed, the frantic night stars moving above me as if the puzzle is being constructed across a universe that has been hidden from most of us, its mighty forces revealed about thirty miles east of El Paso in the middle of nowhere, this vast desert plain interrupted by an ancient umbilical cord cut right here, before me, as the ancient world exploded and fell into itself, surrounding hills and nearby mountains rising over time, challenging the lone rock climber to quit ascending because the desert night is about falling, not rising. The desert night is about having to totter on the edge of things, in order to keep my balancing act and be able to get into my car and manage the dirt roads back to town because night radiance is also about finding a rare, semiprecious gemstone known as peridotite or precious green olivine. This gem lies mostly on the inner eastern and northern slopes of Kilbourne above the rimrock and is found in sizes from crumbly rock to the size of one's fist. Many collectors come here to find softball-sized chunks that, when broken open, reveal the semiprecious olivine. Besides this green olivine, there are rusty reds, gold, purples, brown and black forms of the gem. In the middle of the desert night, I want to bend down and grab a handful of gems from here, but I have never taken anything from the ground in decades, those younger shadows of youth having collected fossils from everywhere. Yet, as I stand near my car and listen to the great silence of nothing overtaking the crater, I want to see a glistening layer of precious rocks before me and find the strength to grab them in my fist, pound them against the car door to ignite them further, watching them glow as a guide out of here. I bend to my knees near the hood of my car and recall the tarantula I spotted here twenty-seven years ago, the sudden headlights catching it as it ran under the black rocks. This time, the bristling shooting stars above me keep me from grabbing a fistful of black sand or illuminating the edge of the crater with my car. As I stated before, it has to be the blindness of approach, brief repose, then retreating in the night without climbing down. It is the complete movement of the night across this geologic grave that lies open to anyone who takes the time to descend. As I prepare to leave, my headlights will blaze, momentarily, and I might see what has been taken from me. Yet, it will be a temporary guiding torch out of this very brief visit to an old sinking, a dry point in the desert that bridges the night with memory—a scant visit that is not made for understanding but to think I can ward off the night and still be granted a black gift. But, to receive it, I must gather the strength to finally open my eyes and adjust to a darkness that has been trying to catch up with me for years.

NIGHT FOLKLORE IN NEWFOUNDLAND AND LABRADOR

PHILIP HISCOCK

When the electric lights came, many Newfoundlanders said in the 1960s, the ghosts and fairies disappeared. You still hear that—or you do if, like me, you regularly engage people in conversation about such things.

Of course, it wasn't quite that simple. But in the same era rural electrification was completed in Newfoundland and Labrador, the common folklore seemed to change, much of it disappearing in some communities. A similar process had occurred throughout North America, but in Newfoundland the tide of European-based folklore had flowed longer, and its ebb happened at least a generation later.

Ghosts and fairies weren't the only casualties—the Christmas nighttime custom of mummering, and the leisure-time customs of telling stories, especially the long, magical "Jack Tales," also were in apparent decline forty years ago. Of course, ghosts and fairies are fruits of storytelling; with electricity came radio and television, and it was they who were the real enemies of storytelling, reducing the very cultural contexts in which telling thrived.

Today at the beginning of the twenty-first century, many of those stories still exist, as does mummering, but both customs are far less popular than they were sixty years ago. Nonetheless, it is not true that no one sees ghosts and fairies—it has even been suggested there was a renaissance of fairy belief in the last quarter of the twentieth century. But the local worlds did change with electric lights.

The conservative nature of contemporary folklore, in whatever era, has been pointed out by every generation of folklorists since the Grimm brothers two hundred years ago. But the worlds we have lost hang around in surprising ways. As much as, and as quickly as, the world around us changes, folklore—vernacular culture—remains an agent of conservation. An exciting thing for folklorists like me has been the tension between the performance of the old and the counterprocess of individuals' creative forces. The latter is folklore's propensity to pick up new stuff along its way. For me as an academic child of the twentieth century, folklore offers tantalizing glimpses of a cultural world that existed before my birth. I do not have to believe in fairies to understand the powers of that belief, then and now.

·₊˙

Newfoundland and Labrador were a separate dominion, or country, in the British Empire of nations until 1949 when it joined the Canadian Confederation as that country's tenth province. Although it was closely linked by oceangoing trade and family ties to Britain, Ireland, the northern United States, and—less so—Canada, its technological and cultural modernization was not equivalent to any of those places. It remained a nation with a difference right through its confederation with Canada, and in the first decade of the twenty-first century it still shows a surprisingly traditional culture. It is an interesting region for folklore fieldwork exactly for its strong balance of cultural conservation and creativity.

Among the Old Stuff that continues to have strong daily meaning for many Newfoundlanders is folklore shaped by the world before electrification: the blackness of night is a bit of the pre-twentieth-century world that continues to influence contemporary folklore. Sometimes it shows up in children's folklore (the boogeyman is the best example), but, perhaps surprisingly, it also is retained by scattered small groups of adults.

·₊˙

Nevertheless, throughout Newfoundland it is a commonplace that —nowadays—most people never see ghosts or fairies anymore because we have the electric lights. Sometimes said with the ironic twist that such things are no longer imagined, it is just as often said as a straightforward explanation—the lights have scared off the non-human beings. But folklore, either positive or negative, is never a universally accepted idea; the belief in fairies, and in ghosts, is probably as strong today as in previous generations. Ten percent of my first-year students at university regularly tell me they believe in fairies. Despite the lighter night skies.

The aurora borealis, the northern lights, is an important part of the folklore especially of the northern half of the province, Labrador. Being less developed and populous than Newfoundland, Labrador retains dark skies and the lights have become part of the artistic output of the region. Visitors from more-lit places learn it is unlucky to whistle at them, and hear stories of unlucky people who did anyway. And they buy framed photographs by local artists as iconic representations of that powerful play of natural light and color in the dark.

·₊˙

At the confluence of Arctic currents and the Gulf Stream, eastern Newfoundland and its waters are especially prone to fog. At night, if no fog, the dark sky provided very explicit, if indirect, maps for travelers. Children learned the basics of the night sky very early, if only to find their way from neighbors' homes: the Big Dipper, the North

Star, and the Maiden Vein (the Milky Way) being the first lessons. But fog, too, even in daytime, is a kind of night that forces the use of certain sensory extensions like weighted twine to sense the depth of water, and to "feel the bottom"—distinguishing sandy bottoms from rocky ones, sloping ones from ledgey ones, and so on. Headlands and "barren" lands (those without trees) were marked with piles of stones known as "marking men" to guide night and fog travelers who could discern their shapes against the horizon, where there might be some viewable contrast. At the beginning of the twentieth century a whole class of valorized local heroes were the men who could find their way without maps, especially at night or in fog.

Newfoundland's cultural roots are largely in two areas of the southern British Isles—small areas around the Irish city of Wexford and the English city of Poole. The English West Country particularly provided some nighttime lore that remains strong. On the night of the longest day of the year, the shortest night of the year, traditionally observed on St. John's Day, June 24, single women and girls would carry out rituals to learn something about their future husbands. Letters of the alphabet might be cut from a newspaper or a disused book, thrown onto the water in a pail, and then left overnight. The night would rearrange them and, next morning, those letters facing up would suggest initials or even spell out the name of the lucky man. Alternatively, the girl could break an egg that night into a glass of water. At first light next morning, she would investigate the eggy forms made by the short but powerful dark; perhaps she would see the masts and sails of a ship, or a blackboard and desk, or the inside of a well-stocked shop, indicating a sailor, a teacher, or a shopkeep as her match. I do not know of anyplace in North America where these Midsummer's Night rituals were preserved with such vigor.

Most of North America did not preserve any of the traditional Bonfire Night celebrations of the home communities of the immigrants who populated them. Newfoundland is an exception in that two strong traditions kept alive a series of fire rituals nearly into the present. In a few Irish-settled communities, the June 24th bonfire tradition continues to this day. More widely, the November 5th bonfire night tradition (known sometimes as Guy Fawkes Night, but certainly predating Fawkes's life) is carried on. Bonfires were not the only form: a variety of fire customs was known around the island: names like Torch Night, Tarmop Night, and the like indicate the methods. In one community old shoes were nailed to sticks, dipped in cod liver oil, and caught alight to be carried through the community. In another town, Tar Barrel Night was when teenaged boys and young men would fill disused half-barrels, formerly used for tar, with kindling. Holding them on their shoulders, pairs of fellows would run through the town until they could no longer carry the burning barrels.

Before electrification, such fire festivals were important parts of the yearly round of custom and entertainment. A woman who grew up in a Trinity Bay community in the 1920s and '30s told me it was a beautifully eerie sight to see a line of flickering lights quietly snaking down over nearby hills toward her town, and a thrillingly dangerous sight to see the boys run through the town with their torches and flaming barrels.

But the thrill of carrying a flaming, oiled boot on a stick is greatly diminished when overhead electric lights are spaced every hundred feet. What were varied and local fire festivals of the early twentieth century—if they have continued at all—almost without exception became homogenous community bonfires by the end of the twentieth century. Even those bonfires are increasingly controlled by municipal regulation and oversight.

Along with electricity and governmental regulation of traditional customs came a kind of homogeneity that reduced the former opportunities for local and personal creativity. The dark, like any obstacle in people's way, gave special strengths to its overcomers, strengths that were valued in their time. Today, for most of us, the dark is no special barrier, particularly where we have all but destroyed it; those "strengths" are seen as poor cousins to modern thrills, technologies, and entertainments. Most children no longer see any immediate value in learning the basics of the sky above their head if they never need to look up, and see a limited subset of what their grandmothers saw. Bonfires, midnight rituals, dusk and dawn fears—all these "texts" of another era's culture have become meaningless now that there is little or no effective difference between day and night. "As goes context, so goes culture" might be a maxim of contemporary folklore studies. In dark's decline, we lost a potent cultural context; today, we certainly see the loss of human abilities that were, not very long ago, much more widespread and valued than they are today.

THE SEVEN STORIES OF NIGHT

SHAUN T. GRIFFIN

I

For seven nights they have sat in the refuge of stars: those hints of white and blue that spend their light in years I cannot explain—the time it takes to travel to my son's eyes. And we remember the ancient wisdom: the earth is part of a celestial body, but tonight we pretend to be its center, separated from the universe, and there are only three of us upon which those stars sink their radiance.

In these few nights their light has bloomed in the burnt offering of sage fire on this mountain below the sun. There has been a kind of weather too, a weather for receiving light, even the light of a star: the dust clouds have parachuted into another backyard and left us with the panorama of night sky. All this has touched the atmosphere, and my sons report that some other light appears to sweep the sky.

II

I gather my sons for the spectacle. We lie on the grass and swim in the phosphorescence of starlight. The younger one points at Orion.

He thinks it looks like a lazy church. We draw lines between the points of Cassiopeia, wade in its mother gaze for the stronger light. We hold pickup sticks overhead, connect the stars, but the boys protest: "They won't stay up there." I laugh and we carefully return them to our noses. The wires are connected—each light a story of the old men who sneak up on us when we lie down. These are the ones we listen for—the deep voices that were once stars. The mobiles of fascination edge into the yard just before dawn. They have come before, they have watched us lie on the damp ground. Once they asked the older boy for water. He could not answer the glints of sleepless understanding.

III

Occasionally I recline on the steps outside my door. I wish that something were holy beyond the purple weight of the horizon. Some light not named, some death of day that is redolent of the other place, the old room in the sky. My first love is up there, drinking, and reading lines from a poem. She says it is about the day before the dark descended and she had to leave, had to find her way to the blue after, and then she closed the door and it is hard to see her except on certain nights when there is an outline that I mistake for her, a collage of stars that looks like a foot or even like her, alone, on the balcony of misgiving. I want to touch her, move into the room with her, want to go up the stairwell and see who it is she is drinking with, reading to, but she cannot tell me, only elaborates on the silence. And then she is lying on her side, book in hand, smiling in the light to come.

IV

The outside of her room is a cage of light with one window, which I have never seen her open. I have seen her silhouette behind the glass, and it is always slumped away from the opening, that infinite sadness she becomes when we are not looking: the night that will not accommodate her supplications, the night of mythology, and then

I am comforted by what I cannot see—the rim of a woman who seems ancient. One by one, I gather stars around her, put them at her feet like wildflowers, and then turn the slightest turn and make yet another bouquet. All this to become a refuge of night, a presence that doesn't have location. It is little more than a tribe of light, an arabesque all about her room. And she may or may not be there. She may be in the anterior, awash in daylight and nearly bright as the dawn, or she may be the riddle between light, the prescient glow of tomorrow, and then of course, she may be gone. I may never see her again, but I try not to believe such because there is holy in the room and it is she. When I cannot look any longer I turn away, bequeath my silence to the last line she read and return to this lit landscape where I confide to the stars.

V

The boys have told me the stars are white stones, flecks of granite floating in the sky. They gather them on a necklace and wear them out to dinner, and when we return they hang them on Saturn's rings. Yesterday the younger boy told me someone took the necklace and threw it across the black outfield. A giant bird knocked it down and held the necklace in his wings. Then he tipped it to the middle of the dark and dropped each star to my boy's hand. He could not understand what the bird was giving him. It must have been hot, must have been a special gift because there is a print in his palm: a starfish without any feeling, an outline of one falling too far. He showed me the pentagon, how it became wedged in his hand without any room for love or drawings. It was the only symbol that he could not wash off. And then he wanted it to leave, wanted me to take the light from him.

VI

After the light of the few streets disappears, I wait for the onset of another sky, the dormant one that will not yield to pressure from below. I am told others wait for this moment to undress this day that turns in parallel: the most quiet forest of night. There is a hole where the picture starts on the east rim. It is a portal, and we cannot resist its emptiness, its hollow exterior. My boys tell me they cannot find it, but I remind them that she is up there too, and if we look hard, she may come to the door. The borders fall away, and one by one we go through the opening, and tonight it is a field of jasmine light, so we embrace it and look at her room. The aperture widens but they do not get scared. They want to stay, want to move beyond this field, into her arms. She turns from us and offers nothing but the temptation of more light. The boys are unsettled. They want to leave the place of stars now. She retreats from the door. On the way back I stop to look, but they pull me and we stand outside while the wind cuts other holes in the sky.

VII

My younger son finds the conical shape in the yard. "A stone has fallen," he says. It is dusk and the birds do not understand this offering. There is a piece of ashen rock nearby. He is poking it and it conforms to his touch. He asks who sent us the white stone and I do not answer. There is a bone beneath the stars, a limb on which they gather strength. Perhaps it has broken off, fallen to us on this imperfect summer night. Perhaps this stranger is one of the stars from the necklace and Saturn sent it to perish in the grass, and then it folds to dust. The young boy traces the impression, a template of four cones and one that fell away. We cannot see the ash any longer. He wants to know if it will be there when we wake, wants me to keep it for him in his drawer. I laugh, thinking of how big this house must be, the house with a star in a drawer. There is no portal tonight, and she has left her room. A bird dips from the tree limb and buries its beak in the dust. Tomorrow the star will be a stone of no origin. And the stone will release its grief.

NOCTURNE WITH MOTHS

ROBERT MICHAEL PYLE

"Maaar-tiiin!" The mother's voice, more exasperated than angry, hung on the evening air. "Come on home, son. It's time you got inside." But as far as her son was concerned, it was never too late to be out.

For Martin Greenstock, the night was always the best time. As early as he was allowed, he stayed outside well into the mellow Denver dusk. He and his big brother, Toby, stalked the alleys of their old neighborhood with a bag of gnawed-on spareribs after dinner, tossing them over fences to all the dogs on their route, on the monthly or so occasions they dubbed "Dog Day." When a little older, they roamed the streets of their raw new subdivision at the edge of the plains, now and then breaking into the Tarzanian falsetto ululation that they designated "the call of the Catman." From there it wasn't long until Jackie Wilson's "Night" on the AM radio station resonated directly with his developing gonads. Van Morrison's "Here Comes the Night," Bob Seger's "Night Moves," and Bruce Springsteen's "Because the Night" and "Something in the Night" would reinforce those dusky sympathies in years to come, cement that tug in the gut that every nocturnal animal knows. And when he walked the streets in the springtimes of high school, sniffing the sweet scent of maturing Hopa crab apples on the warm air and psyching himself up for the morrow's track meet; or cruised the backroads of Arapahoe and Adams counties on his green Allstate Vespa motor scooter, inhaling the heartbreaking tang of cut wheat and hay, well, that was it: by then Martin had been irrevocably recruited to the legions of the night.

His parents seldom worried. In those days, there was nothing unusual about boys—or even girls—possessing a kind of "freedom of the day": after their light chores were done, "Bye, Mom, see you at dinner" was a common salutation. And after dinner, even deep into dimity, neighborhood games of hide-and-seek kept the kids out-of-doors. No one worried about abductions then. True, a few of the lads took advantage of the lack of a curfew to indulge in vandalism and light larceny, but the dark side of darkness never held any charm for Martin, beyond the possibility of meeting girls out late. Happily, one of his chief daylight delights carried over past twilight. Like many a kid in those pre-video days, he'd caught bugs, first in a jam jar and then in nets of his own device. By the age of eleven, butterflies netted most of his attention. It didn't hurt that, unlike the birds with which he'd briefly flirted, they tended to get up late, as was his own summertime wont. He learned the local species well, and occasionally thrilled to a novelty that evoked the interest of serious lepidopterists at the museum and the university, who served as his mentors.

Most of his friends preferred sports or scouts to chasing bugs, but one of his classmates, Dominick Richards, was intrigued. He fashioned his own net and tagged along. The two built up their collection together, using it for show-and-tell, and later as an easy A for their science project. But it didn't take more than two or three summers for Martin and Dominick to collect most of the species common to their locality, and for lack of greater scope, their interest began to wane. One early autumn Saturday, Dominick showed up with his brother's twenty-two instead of his net. "Come on, man," he said. "Grab your BB gun and let's go see what we can find." They walked out along a railroad line past town. Each time they spotted a can or a bottle, they set it up on the rails, then popped it off with a BB or a bullet. "Heck, you couldn't hit an elephant point-blank," said his friend, after Martin's poorly sighted Daisy missed a few times. Dominick seldom missed with his little twenty-two; but then he was the better netsman, too.

"What the heck is THAT?" shouted Martin, as what looked like a big black-and-white butterfly flashed out of a nearby clump of scrubby cottonwoods beside the tracks.

"What?" said Dominick, irritated. "You made me miss!" But then he saw the mystery insect. When it landed on a rabbitbrush, Martin sited, took a shot, and actually hit it. The wings and fat body exploded into a puff of scales and green guts.

"Not much of a specimen," Martin said, as he recovered the shreds.

"But it's *cool*," said Dominick. And look! It's a *moth*!" They could tell by the big, feathery antennae. They ran home, grabbed their nets, came back, and as a September chill and wind arose, they collected a series of the beautiful beasts. Later, Martin bicycled to the downtown library and checked out a crumbling copy of W. J. Holland's magisterial but long out-of-date *Moth Book,* where he learned that their animal was the Nevada buck moth. Again and again that year he took out the book, until his dad finally bought him a secondhand copy of his own. Holland's narrative "Sugaring for Moths," detailing the time-honored technique of attracting choice moths with a treacly mixture of rotten fruit, molasses, stale beer, and rum, enchanted the boys and inspired them to try it for themselves the next summer. Dominick swiped a six-pack of his father's Coors. They put two in the mix with Mrs. Greenstock's brown sugar and overripe bananas, and drank the other four. "Seems fair to me," Dominick burped. They didn't find as many species of bright-striped underwings on their Colorado cottonwood trunks on the high plains as Holland had in the eastern deciduous forest, but enough of the crimson-banded catocalas showed up to keep their attention. "Oho, my Beauty!" they extolled each time they jarred one, mimicking Holland's rich, old-fashioned language.

Another musty treasure from the library, Gene Stratton Porter's *Moths of the Limberlost,* depicted such wonders as luna, polyphemus, and cecropia moths (the latter she called "the Robin Moth") in her own hand-tinted photographs—murky, silky portraits of almost unimaginably alluring night flies. It hadn't escaped Martin's notice that scaly-winged lepidopterans occupied the dark side of the day as well as the sunlight hours, but could such as these really be *real*? Then an amateur collector he knew, a pipe fitter who worked the graveyard shift so he could hunt butterflies by day and didn't care about moths, gave Martin a shoebox crammed with ancient, faded specimens of these giant silkmoths. Bewitched, he resolved to collect his own examples, and to rear them through all their life stages. His first attempt, a batch of cecropia eggs he'd ordered from Michigan, ended with Mrs. Greenstock's distinct displeasure. When the BB-like eggs hatched into hundreds of voracious larvae, apple green and studded with improbable red and blue tubercles, and Martin tired of feeding them one by one, he released them onto his mother's lilacs—which they promptly defoliated.

For Martin and Dominick, moths took over where butterflies left off. Among their greatest thrills was haunting those very lilacs, once they'd recovered, at dusk. There, after early spring rains, they would find migratory white-lined sphinx moths and newly hatched, bright golden owlet moths taking the sweet nectar. Borrowing Holland's lingo, they called these "prizes." It didn't take the boys long, however, to realize that the best way to collect moths was around lights. At first they plucked the brightest and oddest specimens—pink-patched tiger moths, gray *Tolype* with muffs like white rabbit fur, teensy plume moths with wings divided like combed feathers—from their own porch lights, front and back. And once they approached a creepy farmhouse, legendarily occupied by a witch, because of its huge old lilacs and swarms of moths in the screened porch. The "witch" surprised them from behind and scared them silly. "Go ahead, take 'em all," she said, "I don't need 'em." After they'd regained their wits and filled their killing jars, they found lemonade and cookies waiting for them on the porch.

Eventually, Dominick, more adept with girls as well as guns and nets, drifted off to other nighttime pursuits of his own. As for Martin, he began ranging farther afield, high-grading the best moths from porches up and down Racine, Salem, and Scranton streets as well as his own Revere. It was only the innocence of the times, his neighborhood notoriety as the "bug boy," and the local policeman's tolerance that kept him from arrest or worse for repeated trespass.

Even so, he did not fail to cause some alarm among householders, so he took to working the window lights of the nearby shopping center. He liked to walk over there in any case in the ever-springing but almost never met hope of meeting girls, so he took to surreptitiously carrying a collecting bottle in his back pocket. Too often the prime specimens could not be reached without a net, and by now carrying a butterfly net had become socially penalizing, especially at night, so all too often the best bugs remained beyond his reach.

Until, that is, Martin Greenstock came into possession of his own light trap—an ultraviolet contraption with powerful batteries that could be set up in front of a white sheet to attract scads of moths of many kinds. And in fact Martin did believe, like most folks, that moths were actually attracted to lights. It was only later, in graduate school, that he would learn from Professor Covington the truth: extremely sensitive to the least amount of light, especially UV, moths actually become *bedazzled* by bright sources of illumination—circling into the flame, the bulb, the lamppost, the wall, the sheet, or the trap beneath it, and often unable to extract themselves from the beam, as if it were a powerful gravitational field and they, lead shot instead of airy fliers. So "hanging a sheet" or "setting out a light," often in the company of other moth-ers he met through the Lepidopterists' Society, became Martin's passion. He found opportunities to travel to those eastern woodlands described by Holland, luxuriating in full sheets beautifully peppered with the pinks, purples, and yellows of imperial and rosy maple moths, the russets and olives of rare regal moths, and hundreds of others. And when he made it deep into the Central American tropics, and the sheets dripped with so many moths of so many colors and forms, the full scope of natural diversity finally hit home with him. How to choose among this embarrassment of riches?

In order for his light sheets to function well, Martin learned, the conditions mattered. The nearness of undisturbed natural habitats helped, of course. One also went out at the dark of the moon when possible, for the number and range of moths at light were always greater then. But what really seemed to make or break a mothing expedition, Martin discovered, was the amount of artificial light in the night sky.

One postmidnight ten years after the day of the buck moths, Martin Greenstock and Dominick Richards were sitting by a small campfire in the canyon country of eastern Utah. Dominick, after running through college, an early marriage, and a few extreme sports, and missing his old field companion, had come along to see whether maybe moths were the ticket after all. They were running a light in hopes of collecting a few females of Glover's silkmoth for Martin's hybridization experiments. He was sipping a Latter-day Lager and checking the sheet. "You know," Martin said, "when we used to go over to the shopping center as kids, there were tons of moths. I went by there the other night, stopped to check it out, and there were almost none."

"Damn right," said Dominick, tipping his Evolution Amber in the eerie glow of the ultraviolet. "Even I notice that."

"It's the same out in Lakewood," Martin went on. "Of course, most of the nearby habitat is gone."

"That's true," said Dominick. "It's all under houses and asphalt. And then there's all the sprays."

They pondered this for a moment as Martin popped a Polygamy Porter for himself and a St. Provo Girl for Dominick. Then he said, "But it's more than that. Even on the edge of town the moths are way down . . ."

"That's because there *is* no edge of town," Dominick interrupted. "Denver runs into Arvada runs into Broomfield runs into Boulder."

"Right. You have to get halfway to Ward before you get anything much besides army cutworms and *Agrotis ypsilon*. You saw what it was like in Salt Lake—might as well be noon at midnight. Bet you can't find a single *Catocala* below Parley's Canyon."

"It's all one big sea of lights," Dominick sighed.

"Well, I think that's it," Martin went on. "All the damn lights. A little light, or just a few strong lights, can be great for collecting, like when the shopping center was about the only bright spot for miles, or a gas station out in the desert. Or up at Breckenridge Lodge . . . when it was all by itself, you could see the moths come in to the lights by the parking lot, and the bats coming after them, watch the moths' evasive actions and how often the bats hit or missed. But once the ski area grew up into a town and the lights blasted out the night, both the bats and the moths were gone."

"Like every ski town in this damn state. Look at Crested Butte for godsakes . . . or Steamboat!" The two went on in this vein until the first big *Hyalophora gloveri* came spiraling into the sheet, then remembered why they were there.

·.*

Back at the University of Florida that fall, Martin Greenstock's suspicions were confirmed when his professor asked him to take part in a group effort to collect, mount, classify, and analyze light-trapped samples of moths from the rural hinterlands of Gainesville and from a standard suburban site. The former habitat, with its still-dark night skies, yielded hundreds of species and thousands of individuals; the latter location, though it retained many of the same kinds of plants, gave up less than one percent of the moths of the rural site, in both numbers and kinds. The one big difference between the study areas was their relative lightage. That study inspired Martin to focus his own thesis research on the impact of artificial lighting on moth abundance and diversity, which he modeled to show major trickle-down impacts on both bat and songbird populations. He found that hooding streetlights and other high-wattage sources of light pollution could reduce the impact; and that unbridled illumination not only interfered with successful moth courtship, interrupting phero-mone-driven night flights of potential mates, but also prevented females from making it safely to their host plants to lay their eggs. Too, birds learned to congregate around bright lights by morning to prey on the moths sucked in by night. He'd noticed this long ago around his own sheets, and learned to disperse moths he did not collect before pulling the switch and leaving the site.

The summer after Martin finished his PhD, the Lepidopterists' Society held its annual meeting at the McGuire Center for Lepidoptera and Biodiversity, Martin's home throughout his post-graduate studies. He presented the results of his research at the meeting, and found that the experience of many members mirrored his own results. As with amphibian decline, moth losses owed to many factors—insecticides including mosquito fogging, overzealous *Bacillus thuringiensis* application for gypsy moths, biocontrol agents run amok on native species (such as alien flies that parasitized his beloved giant silkmoths), global warming in the High Rockies, habitat alteration almost everywhere. But nothing, it seemed, could compete with the disorientation of bright lights for knocking out the beneficial *Nachtfalters,* as the Germans called them to distinguish them from the *Tagfalters,* the other *Schmetterlingen.* And this was important: people seemed to care about butterflies, which are really just a minor group of day moths. But the much more diverse night moths? Most folks didn't give a rip about them. Because of the bad rep of clothes moths, Martin wondered? Or cutworms in the garden? Or was it just the night? Not everyone loved the night, and its denizens, as he did.

·.*

That summer, Martin was again lighting for moths with Dominick Richards, this time in a northern larch swamp. They were looking for *Hyalophora columbiana* to cross with the *H. gloveri* he had successfully reared from their previous expedition. It seemed the pheromones of several species of giant silkmoths were close enough chemically that they easily hybridized if they came into contact. The moths solved this by occupying different sectors of the dusk, dawn, and the night in between, females of each species "calling" for the males by releasing clouds of pheromones during a given interval. Martin hoped to get a handle on how light pollution might be affecting this delicate clockwork, perhaps threatening the moths further by promoting unhelpful levels of hybridization in nature. The mosquitoes were as thick on their arms as scales on a moth's wing, so they retreated to the cab of Dominick's van and opened a couple of warm Leinenkugels.

"At least out here, it's nice and dark," said Dominick.

"Getting hard to find," Martin agreed, "and now we know what it means; we're not just guessing in the dark, as it were."

"Thanks to your hard work, eh, buddy?" Dominick clicked his bottle to Martin's.

"More thanks to Charlie Covington putting me onto that study," said Martin. "Not that it was happy work. Nothing like documenting the losses of our philistine excesses."

Dominick, who worked for a venture capitalist, said only, "Don't remind me."

"The thing is?" said Martin. "We're in an energy crisis, right? Fossil fuels are past peak, biodiesel takes more energy than it makes, nuclear is damaged goods, hydrogen is smoke and mirrors, solar and wind are minor, dams are coming down for salmon, and big new hydro is DOA. You know what could solve half of the energy needs of the whole damn country overnight, and I mean overnight?"

"What?" asked Dominick.

"Turn off half of the goddam lights!" Martin said. "Or cut their wattage by half." Knowing he was right, he opened two more beers with impotent, but satisfying, pops.

.•*

A few nights later, the two collectors were driving through what used to be nice habitat not far from Itasca State Park. Now there was an auto lot on the edge of an expanding burg, with huge lights blotting out the dark for acres around. "You know what I wish I had at times like this?" asked Martin.

"I'd like a ball-peen hammer for all those super halogen headlights and those damned bogus foglights," said Dominick, who especially hated how blinding headlights had become in recent years.

"Good start," said Martin. "Whack those god-awful blue ones first, for me. But beyond that, then what?"

"A twenty-two?"

"Better yet," he went on. "Remember the first Harry Potter movie, when Dumbledore comes to rescue Harry from the Muggles? He uses a beam from his wand to turn off each streetlamp in the neighborhood as he approaches the house. Remember the sound? '*Beeeoooooowmp!*' And then—sweet darkness! What I wouldn't give for a tool like *that!* Like the units they really do sell, that you can use to turn off TVs in airports and bars, you know?"

"Right," said Dominick. "Well, it would be a boon for burglars, anyway."

"And for the moths."

"There isn't any such tool, right?" asked Dominick, who was pretty sure there wasn't. "Can't buy it on the shopping channel, or in the Sky Mall?"

"Not yet," said Martin. "But just wait."

"Why wait?" said Dominick.

"What do you mean?" asked Martin.

"I've got my twenty-two," said Dominick.

There were six quick pops in the night, not much louder than beer bottles opening. And as the old van rolled away with tungsten headlights dimmed, sweet darkness was restored to one small part of the night.

PART FOUR

THE PLACE WE LIVE HALF OUR LIFE

Just in terms of time, night is half our life. For some, the experience of night may be like that of Gretchen Legler, who in "Acquainted With the Night" reflects on living in "one of the darkest places on the map of the United States." But most of us live in cities and towns amid the wash of artificial light. So, how to value natural night—and why? Counterintuitively, perhaps it's our experiences in cities and towns that teach us to appreciate the value of darkness even more than we might elsewhere. In "The Sound of Falling Snow," Anne Matthews links the qualities of silence and darkness. In "Night Vision," John Tallmadge desires to "teach my children the fruits of night vision and the faith to practice it anywhere, even in the midst of cities." Gary Harrison's "Night Light" shares his story of actively fighting and living with light pollution in his home city. The city is Mark Tredinnick's subject as well, but in "Original Country" he sees it through the lens of his experience living in the Australian bush. And, in "Night in Mind," it is William Fox's experience of night—and non-night—in places as remote as the Arctic and Antarctic, that gives him perspective on city life, and allows him to admit that "my fear is not of the night anymore, but of losing it, because then we would have no way to know our place."

ACQUAINTED WITH THE NIGHT

GRETCHEN LEGLER

I

On a trip once to Bailey Island, across the waters of Casco Bay from Portland, Maine, my partner, Ruth, and I amused ourselves by sitting on the spacious wooden porch of the inn where we were staying, rocking back and forth in high-backed rocking chairs with woven seats, gazing out into the gathering dark. We could see the city of Portland from where we sat, aglow on the horizon, and we could see the light of the ferryboat, the *Scotia Prince,* which carried passengers from the Portland docks north to Nova Scotia, where one could then get another ferry and go even farther, to Newfoundland. The lights of the big boat bobbed and blinked in the distance. The night ocean was so close that the waves crashing against the rocks sent foam spraying over the porch railing and into our faces. Later, she and I went out for a night walk along the road bordered by pink, fragrant beach roses and wild bayberry. A wedding reception was taking place in the main lodge of the inn, and a tired-looking, perhaps slightly drunk man, dressed in a cream-colored suit, his tie loosened at the neck, had come out for some air. He was smoking a cigarette, leaning against his car, his head craned so far back that his Adam's apple and neck exposed themselves in a vulnerable white arc. As we passed, he spoke to us breathlessly, like a child having just made a discovery. He couldn't contain himself. "There are so many stars!" he said. We asked him where he was from. New Jersey, he said. "You can't see them from where I live." We left him with his head tilted dangerously back, gazing awestruck, upward, his cigarette tip glowing orange in the dark.

Maine is one of the darkest places on the map of the United States of America. It is mostly trees, rocks, water, wild creatures, hills, and sky. Islands and bays dot the eastern and southeastern edges of the land. Rolling blueberry and potato fields, swamps, lakes, ponds, and still great swaths of maple, oak, pine, and hemlock cover the interior. Only 1.2 million people live in Maine—41 persons for every square mile of land. The state is tenth from the bottom in the nation's population lineup. A look at the Maine map shows a moderately peopled coastline, a somewhat lesser-peopled southern and western interior, and all that fading slowly into wilderness in the north—to Mount Katahdin, to the Allagash, to millions of acres of logging land owned predominantly by paper companies, but slowly being developed into huge "wilderness" subdivisions where the wealthier among us might purchase second or third homes, perhaps a time-share condominium on Moosehead Lake; a place to escape the nation's sprawling cities with their invasive lights and incessant noise. For now, at night Maine is as dark as the Rockies, as dark as the Great Lakes, as dark as the deserts of the West. Portland, with its 230,000 residents, is the biggest metropolis in Maine; it is home to a quarter of the state's residents, and, so far, the only city big enough to disturb this darkness.

III

My partner and I live on eighty acres of woods in the hilly region of western Maine. In the beginning, the forest pressed so close to the house that we had hardly any sunshine for our weedy lawn, full of wild strawberries, dandelions, and wildflowers; no sun for our perennial flower beds or our vegetable gardens, and our houseplants suffered even in the windows. After a few years of trimming back the forest, which provided us with enough firewood to keep us warm during three winters, we now are surrounded by a small log and stump-filled "meadow" where our goats graze, and beyond that, a still-thick woods full of maple, oak, birch, beech, hop-hornbeam, ash, and more. Our house is a small cape, with a steep roof, a door in the middle, and a window on each side. You reach the house via a curving stone pathway. It is the kind of house you might expect a child to draw at school on a big sheet of white paper with crayons, a little curl of smoke snaking up from a redbrick chimney in the center of the roof, a nuclear family holding hands off to the side.

There is a porch light to the left of the granite steps as you approach the house, but we almost always leave it off in the summer, as it attracts moths, mosquitoes, june bugs, and other insects to the door, and when we enter, they slip inside to flutter and bump against the lamp shades and whine annoyingly in our ears as we try to sleep. Instead, on summer nights we approach the house in the dark. We park the car on the dirt and gravel pad at the end of the driveway, and as the light inside the car fades, we are left in near total blackness. As our eyes adjust, the house comes into view, with only the faint glow of the light from the bulb above the stove shining through from the back of the house to the front windows. The large, full-topped beech tree to the left comes into hulking shape, as does the barn at the end of the yard. The gray pathway stones emerge. We walk slowly to the door, carrying an empty bowl, say, from a potluck with nearby friends, or groceries picked up late on the way home, and as we step carefully along the uneven stones, we look up at the sky to see a milky litter of stars unknown to us but also those that are our familiar friends—Ursa Major and Ursa Minor; Polaris, the North Star; in late summer the Pleiades, Taurus, and Orion; earlier in the season Cassiopeia and Cygnus the giant swan.

One June, a friend from New Delhi, India, was visiting us. He had been staying for almost a week already, delighting in helping me till the vegetable garden, plant beans, mow the lawn, drive our pickup truck recklessly in small circles on the grass in front of the barn, collect fresh milk from the farm down the road and from it make delicious, creamy Indian rice pudding with cardamom and raisins. He often took pleasure in teasing us about being vitamin-fed Americans with all the attendant arrogance and privilege of our nationality, race, and class, but in time he softened a bit when he saw how hard we work at growing our own food organically, recycling our paper, cans, and bottles; saving kitchen scraps and lawn clippings for the compost pile. With the farm down the road and the garden in the yard, the life we led had more in common than he had imagined with the lives of others who lived in less-well developed places in the world. One night Sudip and I returned to the house from dinner at a restaurant in nearby Wilton. As we made our way up the dark walk, he stopped for a moment and looked around him, stretching out his hands as if to feel the night. "The night is so black," he said, finally. "So black. This could actually be my boyhood village in Bihar."

IV

In late summer the tall fields of grass surrounding the home of our good friends in nearby Chesterville hum and buzz with insects all day long. The fields are home to milkweed, fern, black-eyed Susan, daisies, sweet pea, clover, and all manner of other tall, waving plants, whose seeds and nectar would be harvested by birds, bees, and butterflies, until fall, when the owner of the land would have his hired man come with a tractor and cut the fields so that they would not become grown over with saplings and blackberry bushes. On the edge of the mown lawn, just where the tall grass begins, our friends have built a sauna from an old chicken coop. We regularly spend evenings there, in the winter and in the summer, bathing companionably, and, depending on the season, leaping out into the fresh snow, or washing off the sweat under a portable shower hung on a nail outside the door. Afterward, we go into the house for supper and stay, usually, until well into the night, talking of the news of the day. On one such night our friend Doug, who had taken the dogs out before they bedded down for the night, called to us urgently: "Everybody outside. Hurry up. Now!" We all jumped to our feet, afraid that part of the house was on fire, or that there had been an accident at the intersection down past their mailbox. Silently, he beckoned us to the front of the house, where we all gathered, and then he gestured for us to look into the nearby field. What we saw there against the dark background of the trees on the far edge of the meadow took our breath away. There were thousands of tiny lights. So thick were the clouds of fireflies that they seemed like illuminated raindrops filling the sky. They flickered on and off, diving and rising, settling on blades of grass, then taking off again, creating great, gentle curlicues of light. The whole field, as far as we could see, all the way back to the stone walls, was glittering, sparkling, shimmering, twinkling. It was enough to make one believe in fairies, or help one imagine why fairies *have been believed in.* The dancing lights. The unexplained luminescence.

V

Early sailors returning from the South Pacific reportedly claimed to have seen fairies. It is believed that what they really saw, however, were fireflies blinking, remarkably, in unison—a still not uncommon phenomenon in that part of the world. The delightful conclusion that the fireflies were fairies is understandable. Most cultures claim some kind of lore that includes fairies. Sometimes the fairies are ugly, sometimes they are evil, most often they are mischievous, as with Celtic fairies such as the pooka, the banshee, and the leprechaun, or the fairies that kidnap human children and replace them with changelings. Sometimes the fairies are the sweet, gauzy, winged helpers with magic wands of Walt Disney fame. Some say that the firefly, with its little blinking light, may have been part of the impetus for J. M. Barrie's Tinker Bell, the magical fairy in the story *Peter Pan.* The diminutive, diaphanous, winged creature that is Tinker Bell became, in the nineteenth century, *the* popular Western image of the fairy. The early twentieth century saw not only Barrie's play (and read the subsequent book), but a number of other popular confrontations about the existence of these tiny beings. The best known is "The Case of the Cottingley Fairies," wherein two young girls captured on film dancing fairies in the gardens and woods near their homes in Yorkshire, England. They had numerous supporters, including Sir Arthur Conan Doyle, the creator of the fictional British sleuth Sherlock Holmes, and a devotee of spiritualism, the then new and popular wave of thinking that included belief in spirits, fairies, ghosts and other unseen beings, and the practice of séances. Well after the original episode in 1917, Elsie and Frances confessed to using paper cutouts to create the images.

VI

For the kind of miraculous magic show that I witnessed outside my friends' home in Maine, these insects, which are really beetles from the large family Lampyridae (meaning "shining ones"), require only four essentials: long grass, trees, and shrubs; an absence of pesticides and herbicides; moisture; and, most of all, darkness—all factors that may be contributing to the absence of fireflies in numerous cities and towns across the nation. The competing shine of porch lights, streetlights, stoplights, automobile headlights, the fluorescent light pouring out into the dark from office towers, the lamplight seeping into the night from suburban picture windows, disturbs and confuses the fireflies. They need to be able to see one another, after all. The light show is a mating ritual: the males fly about, flashing their patterned signals—one-two-three-four-five-pause, one-two-three-four-five-pause—and females, perched on blades of grass or leaves, either respond—one, one, one—or not. There are 136 species of fireflies, each with a different flash pattern, so this conversation in light has to be precise—each male of each species needs to find a female mate of the same species, and often multiple species are flashing and dancing in the same field together. The ritual requires a background of dark. Firefly bioluminescence, the bright glow at the tail, is the result of a reaction between the organic compound luciferin, the enzyme luciferase, and oxygen. Oxygen is the fuel. Luciferin is the source of the light. Luciferase is the trigger. These amazing chemicals have been used in the service of genetic engineering—a glowing tobacco plant one of the signs that animal genes had successfully been transplanted to plants. A chemical company in Ohio has been collecting fireflies for scientific research on cancer, cystic fibrosis, heart disease, and multiple sclerosis. For 75,000 fireflies they will pay you $750, a penny apiece.

VII

From *Peter Pan* has emerged the term "the Tinker Bell effect," an ironic reference to things that exist only because people believe in them. The scene when Tinker Bell drinks the poisoned draught laid for Peter by his nemesis Captain Hook leaves her nearly dead. She can only be saved, she tells Peter, if people believe in fairies. "If you believe clap your hands, don't let Tink die," Peter calls out. There is some hissing, but enough hands clap to bring her back from the brink, whereupon Barrie writes: "She never thought of thanking those who believed, but she would have liked to get at the one who had hissed." The word *fairy* or *fairie* has its origins in Old French and the original Latin word *fata,* or fate—the unseen forces that determine the course of one's life. In Old French *feerie* meant being in a state of *fee*—a state of enchantment. *Fey,* a more modern word, has come to mean to be touched, or slightly of another world.

VIII

When we first moved to western Maine we were taken by surprise at the thick dark. We were struck first by the moonlight. The contrast between the dark of the night and the light of the moon meant that on those nights when the moon was full, or even only partly so, the night shone a ghostly bright—so bright one might have read a novel outside; bright enough to cast lifelike shadows with crisp edges—shadows of trees, their limbs reaching out like the delta of blue veins under the thin skin of a delicate wrist; shadows of blades of grass, intricate fronds of fern, the cupola and weather vane atop the barn, the neighbors' bulky trash cans set out for Friday pickup; shadows of the stone walls that ran along the edges of the roads and fields; shadows from the bean poles, from the tomato plants.

Nothing standing escaped the attentions of the moonlight. In that darkness, lit by moon, one could imagine all manner of dramas taking place—small bloody murders committed by night-roaming housecat upon vole, the banditry of the raccoon feasting on the garden's ripe corn, a child, unable to sleep, gazing from her bed at the magic outside her window, a little enchanted, a little afraid.

IX

One night in the early part of the summer, after we had both fallen deeply asleep, we were awakened, both sitting bolt upright in our beds, by a terrifying scream. Again it came, and again, louder each time. We stepped quickly to the open window thinking we were about to witness a murder. We were so frightened by the noise that I grabbed the baseball bat that stands in a corner beside the bed. The screams began at the back of a throat and gurgled and rose as if caught up in a flow of blood. A friend told us later that the cry in the night came most likely from a fisher—an elusive, large, dark-haired, weasel-like creature known for its ferocity, and its blood-curdling call—either that or a fox marking its territory. There was one final scream that night, then the sound of shuffling leaves, the slight breaking of branches, and whatever unseen thing it was, was gone.

X

The second spring we spent in our house in the woods was the spring of the foxes. We discovered them first when we saw the small, fuzzy fox kits sunning themselves on top of a gray boulder beside the road near the end of our steep driveway. We would drive by, the car window down, staring foolishly, and the fox kits would stare back, their eyes sleepy and lazy and their bodies limp from the warmth of the sun. Once I went to investigate the boulder more closely and found a deep, cool, dark hole dug beneath one end of the rock, a great pile of loose dirt and small bones at the mouth, the inside smelling of roots and earth and wild animal. Later, as the little foxes began to wander farther from home, we would encounter the kits, bigger now and even more delightfully fluffy and red, playing in the driveway—tumbling in the dirt, rolling over one another, biting each other's ears and necks. In the mornings we would find little piles of fox scat on the stone pathway leading to the house, and even on the granite steps at the front door. It excited us, and slightly unnerved us, to think of the foxes out at night, exploring our yard, peering into our windows. One night, before bed, as I was about to shut out the last of the lights and take my tea up to read, I saw a small, fur-rimmed face in the glass beside the door. The face itself was lit by the lights from the room inside, but beyond that, all was dark. I saw perfectly shaped triangle ears still slightly soft around the edges, a black nose at the end of still rounded, puppyish snout, whiskers, and clear eyes in which the last lamplight of the house shone back. I called for Ruth to come and see, but at the sound of my voice the little fox was gone.

THE SOUND OF FALLING SNOW

ANNE MATTHEWS

When the North American power grid faltered in August 2004, over ten million people took to the streets—not to loot or protest, but to gaze, astonished, at the night sky. For a few summer evenings, a postmodern population knew real quiet and true darkness. Reporters in Canada and the United States, seeking tales of horror and hardship, heard instead about the glories of the firmament.

"I could see the stars very clearly, which was rare, and magical."

"Stars like you've never seen in your life. Fascinating and terrifying at the same time."

"No neon, no streetlights, no apartment lights. Peaceful."

"The whole neighborhood sat talking by candlelight, or just listened to the crickets."

"We should have power outages more often."

Since the late 1980s, a global patchwork of individuals and organizations has worked to preserve silence and darkness. Some focus on neighborhoods, others on nations; all hope to protect the commons from unwanted intrusion. It shouldn't take an international power cut, they argue, to let us rediscover starlight and quiet. Maybe such things are, in fact, social capital. A public investment. A cultural heritage. Or even a civil right.

The struggle to keep night dark and nature audible can look quixotic, even doomed, given our high-decibel, high-wattage, 24/7 ways. Yet advocates for night and silence keep advancing their overlapping causes through legal face-offs and Internet lobbying, policy and poetry; preserving a negative, championing an absence. Thirty years ago, skywatchers remind us, dark skies existed within an hour's drive of most major population centers. Today one often needs to travel 150 miles or more. Astronomers amateur and professional gauge the success of such journeys via the Bortle Dark-Sky Scale, which sets nine levels of darkness. At a prime viewing site, starlight from the Milky Way casts shadows on the ground. Truly dark conditions are nearly as good, followed by rural sky, rural/suburban transition, suburban, bright suburban, suburban/urban transition, city sky, and, least rewarding of all, inner-city sky, which can be fifty times brighter than natural conditions.

Likewise, all-natural soundscapes are nearly extinct in North America and Europe, even in remote reserves, thanks to persistent noise pollution by helicopters, snowcats, ATVs, and overflying jets. The Nature Sounds Society, affiliated with the California Library of Natural Sounds in Oakland, has documented such deterioration for decades. As curator and cofounder Paul Matzner explains: "Recordists and others who return time after time to listen to and document previously pristine locations world-wide find that these are fast disappearing under the onslaught of technological sources of noise. We must work now to preserve these places or they will soon be gone. As 'in wildness is the preservation of the world,' so in the quietude of wilderness, we believe, is the preservation of its very essence." One NSS member is Gordon Hempton, an acoustic ecologist who won an Emmy Award for his 1992 documentary, *The Vanishing Dawn Chorus.* In 1984, Hempton knew twenty-one places in Washington State where he could reliably record natural sound for fifteen minutes straight. By 1999, there were only three. If Olympic National Park, he points out, would ever pledge to protect one square inch of silence—an environmental preserve entirely free of human-made sound—it would mean enforcing quiet for hundreds of miles around.

The disenchantment of night has taken two centuries, ever since gaslight first brightened the forges and cotton mills of the British Midlands. Industrial lighting made streets safer, shops and theaters more alluring. Previously, night meant both liberation (thanks to the joys of communal masquerades, parades, and bonfires) and danger (since darkness presumably encouraged mobs, robbers, spirits, and dark magics). Until Benjamin Franklin proposed daylight savings time, early America used the night in serial fashion: a "first sleep" from eight or nine till midnight, then several hours of wakefulness and socializing in the wee hours, followed by a "second sleep" until dawn. But a recolonized night nearly always meant the death of peace and quiet too.

"More and more as the hum and roar and scream of engines grows and closes in, I remember the silence of my childhood and youth," wrote British novelist Lucy M. Boston in 1973. "The present generation has no conception of silence. If it could be imagined it would be the silence of death, not of abounding life. Formerly it enfolded everything. We broke into it and it closed round us again. This gave great interest to sounds when they occurred, lost now since noise is the continuum."

As we steadily banish silence and night, law and culture are again in flux. Noise and light ordinances have long been aimed at individual nuisances, not social prescription; for voters and consumers to demand darkness and quiet requires a sea change as great as the push against drunken driving, or pesticides, or secondhand smoke. "Twenty or 30 years ago," argues Daniel Green, an astronomer at the Harvard-Smithsonian Center for Astrophysics in Cambridge, Massachusetts, "most people didn't smoke, but you assumed you couldn't do anything about it. Now we see it can be changed."

Some city governments think so too. New York's Operation Silent Night goes after chronic, disruptive noise with sound meters, vehicle checkpoints, monitoring at intersections, towing of vehicles, seizure of audio devices, summonses, and arrests. Ottawa and Charleston run special noise-complaint courts. London is cutting Heathrow night flights in response to a European Court of Human Rights ruling that every person deserves a good night's sleep. College towns from Tuscaloosa to Amherst to Lansing have embraced anti-student-noise ordinances. In Fort Lupton, Colorado, at least one judge sentences noise scofflaws to mandatory doses of John Denver, Wayne Newton, and Henry Mancini. (Fort Lupton has *very* few repeat offenders.) And Tokyo is building its newest highways belowground, then placing parks on top, to permit even an expressway's neighbors to enjoy the very Japanese pleasure of *shin-shin,* the sound of snow falling.

A host of interest groups and nonprofits rally and educate, like the Dark Skies Coalition, and Canada's vigorous Right to Quiet Society. The patron of the Campaign to Protect Rural England is the queen, who says she often dreams of retirement in quiet Lancashire. Vermont's Noise Pollution Clearinghouse (motto: good neighbors keep their noise to themselves) keeps a useful list of 20 Noises We Can Do Without, like race tracks, car alarms, volunteer-fire-department sirens, garbage trucks, night flights, air tourism over national parks, jet skis, leaf blowers, commercial air conditioners, boom cars, and cell phones in public places. The archived headlines on its Noise News website are instructive too: "Enraged Neighbors Attack Sacramento Billiard Palace," "Nebraska Good Humor Man Cannot Ring Bells, Says Irate Council," "New Orleans Neighborhoods Ban Leaf Blowers as Worse Than Garbage Trucks at 5 AM," "Helicopter

Noise Declared Public Health Hazard in New York, New Jersey," "Singapore Fines Floor Refinishers; Far Too Noisy."

But progress comes lightbulb by lightbulb, and sometimes light-and-noise debates pit two desirable outcomes, as in rural Somerset, England, where countryside defenders and architectural preservationists have been at odds over the reopening of a historic lime kiln, which would roar twenty-four hours a day to produce the traditional lime mortar so badly needed to restore cathedrals and stately houses. (A retired engineer who lives five hundred yards from the proposed incinerator told the *London Guardian,* "It's just one more nail in the coffin of anyone trying to get a good night's sleep.")

Sometimes we can choose to change, and sometimes biology chooses for us. In the fall of 2004, Mars swung closer to Earth than at any time since Neanderthal days. Skyglow and glare kept most North Americans from seeing our neighboring planet at such close range, brilliant and ruddy though it shone in the evening skies. Many did not look. Others tried and failed. Forty percent of us now live in areas so constantly lit that our eyes never really adjust to night vision. Evolution does not always mean improvement. We are, in every sense, losing our ancient ability to see in the dark.

NIGHT VISION

JOHN TALLMADGE

Most of us learn to fear the dark at an early age. I grew up in the city, right outside New York, in an old Victorian house with a basement straight out of Edgar Allan Poe. Ragged cobwebs hung from the walls, heavy with coal dust and mildew. Old chairs rotted in corners. Creaking doors led to earth-floored closets perfect for casks of amontillado. There was even a monster under the stairs that would leap out the minute you turned off the light. So we played outside, ranging all over the block. Mom let us climb trees and run over garage roofs, but we always had to be in by dark. My father would lock the doors at night, turning the big brass bolts with a reassuring thud. There was no telling who might be roaming around outside, looking for an easy mark. Personally, I knew it was robbers. Some nights I would lie awake formulating escape plans. While they broke in and took my parents hostage, I would climb out the bathroom window and shinny down the gutter, then bolt for our secret passage between the garages; it was too narrow for grown-ups and came out right near the police station. Having a good plan helped me relax. I'd drift off, then act it out in dreams where, somehow, my shoes were always nailed to the floor. I'd awake in panic, feeling the thieves' hot breath on my neck. But it was only the twisted bedsheets and my father snoring comfortably in the next room, regular as a ticking clock in the dark, safe house.

On those city nights I rarely saw the stars, even when we stayed out after dark. My first glimpse of the constellations came indoors, during a show at the Hayden Planetarium, where Zeiss projectors created a sky artificially cleansed of the smoky glow that covered the whole metropolitan area. The constellations appeared in textbook clarity, etched against ghostly images of the creatures and heroes for whom they were named: Scorpio with his raised stinger, Orion with his bow, the fishes of Pisces entwined like yang and yin. How could a few random stars have suggested such rich, intricate images to the ancients? It was too much for a seven-year-old city boy to grasp.

I had an easier time on the drive home, when my father sometimes took us to Eagle Rock for a nighttime view of the city. Here basalt cliffs had been preserved as a county park. They rose dramatically from the settled plain, right behind the labs where Thomas Edison had developed electric light. From the top we could see the fruits of his ingenuity sparkling all the way to Manhattan, which rose like a glowing, jewel-encrusted reef. The landscape at our feet looked like another sky. We could see the violet necklaces of expressways lit by mercury vapor, the orange catenary arcs of suspension bridges, the yellow, rectilinear grids of neighborhoods. Here and there a bright, galactic cluster marked some commercial district or town center, from which feeder streets radiated like spiral arms. Edison's art had created a whole new set of constellations, at once more familiar and alluring than the mythic shapes in the planetarium. In those days, it seemed as if science and industry could actually make a new heaven right here on earth.

But it was one thing to create a thousand points of light and quite another to deal with the spaces between them, where all my old fears still lurked. The brighter the light, the blacker the dark. It was not until summer, when we left for my grandmother's lake house, that I began to look up at the night sky. Hills blocked out the city glow, and on clear, windless nights the black water reflected the full sweep of the Milky Way. My parents and I would sit on the dock watching for meteors or satellites while dim, nocturnal fish rippled the surface and cars growled past on the road, probing with thin, nervous headlights. They had no idea what they were missing. How could anyone fear darkness in such a place, where the bright, unedited sky bristled with countless stars? I had never imagined that night could be so luminous, so clear, so peaceful and refreshing.

And yet, whenever a light appeared, I was infallibly drawn to it. Some nights we'd light a fire on the pier my folks had built from stones hauled out of the lake; we'd cook burgers, sing songs, and tell stories as darkness fell. I loved staring into the fire or watching the light play on people's faces. It was a primeval scene. Sometimes I would arrive late, groping along the dark path, and it always surprised me how entranced people looked. They had no idea I was there, nor what other creatures might be watching. In a hostile world, they'd be vulnerable, fully exposed. It was the same way with the house, floating in the woods like a cruise ship all lit up and packed with laughing relatives. From outside you could study their every move, while from inside all they could see were their own reflections. Some nights I would walk all around before going in, just to see what they were up to. I knew that once inside the bright light would destroy my night vision, and I'd be as blind and clueless as the rest.

On other nights, I'd practice walking without a flashlight, navigating by sound or feel. My feet followed the hump at the center of the drive; the flick of weeds against my ankles steered me onto the sandy path that crunched reassuringly with each step. And soon a cool, faint glow among the trees would open out into the lake itself, with the dock jutting out like a black granite slab against the water. After a cosmic hour, I'd walk back to the house unerringly. The woods hummed with life, but there was nothing there that could hurt me. I knew my way around. I had a head full of starlight. Even in the dark, I could see.

So the country began to dispel my childhood fears. A few more summers, and I was ready for night in the city. Now the view from Eagle Rock promised adventure to young teens stoked with hormones. A short ride took us right into Times Square with its swirling crowds, its pulsing electric billboards and throbbing discos. We shouldered our way past strip-show hucksters and pimps, theatergoers and iron-faced shopkeepers. We gazed after laughing couples as they disappeared into cabs, eavesdropped on clots of tourists gabbling in unknown tongues, shied away from young gangsters sporting gold and tattoos. It seemed as if the whole world were pouring through Times Square. We saw people we recognized from the news, athletes, actresses, even, on one memorable night, Richard Nixon himself striding along in his Republican cloth coat and staring grimly ahead like a true leader of the free world. And all the while, around the shadowy edges of this carnival, well-dressed men were shaking hands across restaurant tables while outside under the streetlamps luminous faces were rising to be kissed. Night in the city was one big masquerade, a kaleidoscope of light and dark that fostered shape-shifting and disguise. You could slip into the shadows and emerge as someone else. You could steal a kiss or an identity. Who would know? It worked like magic. All you needed was a dose of shadow, a simple fix, an intoxicating hit that broke the bounds of your rigid daylight self. The shopgirl would blossom into a femme fatale, the delivery boy into a disco king. And well-bred suburban kids would morph into adventurers on the prowl, sleek, powerful, and dangerous. But the worst thing we ever did was to run all the red lights on the way home, because it was 3:00 AM and there was no one else around. That turned out to be enough of a thrill. The rest was all mystery and imagination.

So between country and city I lost my fear of night, but I learned to love it only years later, on wilderness trips to the western mountains. Hiking for days at high altitude, far from the human world with its clocks and calendars, my body and mind would settle into phase with the planet's diurnal rhythms. I felt myself slipping back into an older world, the one we had been born in and adapted to over hundreds of thousands of years. Each day, as dusk gathered, I could feel my night vision deepen. The stars looked unbelievably close, so numerous they seemed almost to pave the sky. The Milky Way shone like a river that carried the Northern Cross like a floating spar. How cool and serene it felt to bathe my eyes in its ancient light. How many million years had it traveled to reach us, in contrast to the young, hot light of our sun, a mere eight minutes old? I thought of my own species' immense journey and imagined a ray of light leaving some distant star and beaming through space over all that time until, right now, it crashed into my retina, transferring its energy into neural impulses and thereby creating an image that I could see. This was real light, bright with the secrets of the universe. To see it I had to stay out in the dark, waiting with open eyes. It made my Times Square adventures seem like a drug-crazed high.

Night in the city was all about pushing away the dark into corners and alleys, but night in the wilderness let me embrace it. Every patch of city dark was a shadow created by human acts of illumination. But there were no shadows in the wilderness at night. Or rather, it was all one shadow, the earth's own shadow, to be precise, and therefore simply a part of home. I realized then that my childhood fears of robbers or monsters were merely projections of fears and desires I carried within myself. There was nothing in the wilderness that would hurt me. I was more likely to be harmed by my own demons, my own lust, greed, anger, or pride. Imagining these as outside threats meant I could avoid dealing with them inside. Therefore, they could still hide safe and sound and come out at will to dance in the dark whenever I took to living behind locked doors. But there was no hiding in the wilderness, no inside or outside, no walls or electric light.

I soon discovered that night in the wilderness held many other gifts. With the hard clarity of day removed, I learned to pay attention to other senses besides vision, and when I did use sight, to avoid the focused stare. Night vision required short, jerky movements of the head and eyes to detect motion and outline rather than color or fine detail. By day I could fix a position, identify a person or animal moving across a slope, trace a route, or spot a campsite. I could make up my mind and take time to act. But at night identification took longer, and I had to suspend judgment while gathering information from other senses. Smell could reveal who had passed through and how long ago. Touch could sense changes in wind or temperature that might prove useful in choosing where to camp. Hearing could detect presence and movement calibrated by distance and direction. All these required more patience and intimacy than sight. You had to get closer to things in order to recognize them. You had to open yourself, become more sensitive and alert. After many nights I could almost feel my skin growing thinner, pores thirsty for any sensation. I began to slow down, keep still; I began to watch and listen. It was not contemplation, where you lose yourself in the object of regard, but more like the deliberate poise of a dancer, finding the delicate balance point from which all movement begins.

At night in the wilderness, I learned, the self does not disappear under a disguise, clench with fear, or seek control by holding the world at arm's length. Rather, it relaxes, opens, breathes, extends its attention outward into the world the way a plant feels its way into the soil with roots or into the air with leaves. Night teaches you to gather information, suspend judgment, and cultivate what Keats called "negative capability," the capacity to hold conflicting ideas in mind without deciding between them. This faculty serves many ends besides those of poetry and art. It fosters compassion, encourages forgiveness, moderates haste, defuses anger, promotes tolerance, fosters diversity, and catalyzes learning. We need it for healthy relationships; we need it for making peace; we need it to live sustainably and honorably on the earth.

After many nights on the trail, immersed in Paleolithic time, I thought it would be easy enough to bring these lessons home and put them into practice. It was always a shock to return to the human world and find it so filthy and depraved. Sometimes it felt like coming in from a night walk at the lake, craving the human warmth but shrinking back from the stifling blindness of indoor light. Our culture seemed to have fallen in love with its own cheap thrills. I could feel my wisdom evaporate in the glare of civilization. So I had to keep going back with friends or students, struggling to maintain contact with the wild and the light of night through a strenuous, migratory life.

And now, years later, I am a father and a householder raising kids in the city, where, like it or not, most people live and work. It would be so easy if we could just live like the old prophets out in the wilderness fed by the bread of angels. But we can't. We have to achieve some sort of reconciliation, especially when we find ourselves going through the whole process again with our kids: the night terrors, the monsters under the bed, and later, God help us, the passion for reckless adventure. What can I do but try to teach my daughters the skills and virtues of night vision, so that they will be able to manage their own demons in a visually obsessed and benighted age?

We all crave clarity, certainty, and control. Indeed, we define success in such terms. By day, even nature itself seems to serve this desire. How prodigious the daylight is! It floods everything, penetrating into the deepest nooks and recesses of our world. Even hiding in the closet, my kids can see the shoes and dresses lit by the scattered glow from the bright sliver under the door. By day we move through light like fish through the sea: we breathe it, suck it in through our pores, take it completely for granted. The ubiquity and pervasiveness of light make everything stand out in hard-edged clarity. We can read things at a distance and make our plans. We can move without contact, act without immediate consequence, contemplate, envision, strategize, calculate. We can see ahead. But this undeniable power does not come without a cost. Vision allows us to know things only by their surfaces. We can't tell what's going on within; hence, it enables deception and disguise. Surface knowledge can also create a false sense of security. Gazing at people, animals, or landscapes, we can label or objectify them. We can judge or appraise; we can envy, desire, or hate. We can project our own demons onto other beings, so that they become imagined necessities to our own fulfillment. Think how many evils—racism, for example—could be counteracted if people would only *touch* rather than *look*. I don't mean to impugn vision per se, only to warn about how we overprivilege it and are, therefore, more easily led astray. Daylight understanding is not adequate for a wholesome, responsible, and loving relation to the world.

I want to teach my children the fruits of night vision and the faith to practice it anywhere, even in the midst of cities. I want them to experience the Milky Way and the constellations at altitude, in the desert or mountains, so they will know what's hidden by culture's glowing haze. I want them to cultivate negative capability and suspend the rush to judgment. I want them to practice attentiveness, empathy, intuition, and compassion. I want them to understand how pornography trades in slick surfaces and the objectifying gaze. I want them to know how to resist envy and avarice, the glitter of wealth, the chimeras of fashion, the manufactured lusts of advertising and politics.

That's why from time to time I take them outside to sit on the porch as dusk falls on the city. We watch the trees change from intricate green to black silver etched against lavender blue. We watch the fireflies ascend like newborn stars flashing their messages of hope and desire—"Choose me! Choose me!"—while cicadas and crickets sing of love from their hidden perches. If it is very clear we might catch a glimpse of Mars gleaming red as a garnet over the rooftops, or perhaps a meteor or even a comet. We know the Milky Way is up there too, floating the Northern Cross. We can feel the animals coming out and moving under the trees—coyotes, raccoons, possums, and deer emerging to take back the night as the people retreat indoors. In this way, I find, the wilderness always returns. I no longer have to seek it; it comes to me. I want my children to know that it waits for them as well. All they have to do is look beyond the light.

NIGHT LIGHT

GARY HARRISON

One of my earliest and most vivid memories is of the night sky over Hickam Field—the army air base outside of Honolulu—on Oahu. It was February 1954, and my bereaved father, myself, and my sister, only a few weeks old, were flying from Yokohama, Japan, to San Francisco, on our way home after the unexpected death of my mother, who succumbed to an asthma attack in our army quarters—another profound memory. As we stepped out onto the tarmac, I remember looking up into the darkest sky I had ever seen illuminated by innumerable stars. My father had told me that my mother's spirit had joined that visible chorus of twinkling lights, and I was trying to find her from among the thousands and thousands of other souls that I saw looking down upon us.

Perhaps it was that moment that led to my affinity for the night, for the deep darkness that opens up the canopy of stars and planets, the faint clouds of the Milky Way, and the occasional meteor or even meteor shower. It was a meteor, a "falling star," I was seeking on that night as I gazed up into the visible darkness, for my father had said that falling stars were the trails of souls making their way from this world into the great beyond. I wanted to see my mother one more time.

I don't remember seeing a meteor that night. And I was quickly taken into the airfield, where we showered and prepared for the next leg of the flight. We made it to San Francisco, then to western Kansas where I lived in Grinnell, population 315, with my grandparents for a couple of years and then on and off in the summers. In Grinnell, I was equally fond of the sky, despite the corner streetlight poking through the branches of the trees across from the porch where grandpa "Doc" and I always sat at night, sometimes watching lightning on the horizon, at other times hoping for clouds, and always, it seemed, feeling the warm, sometimes hot, breeze brushing across our faces and stirring the leaves on the trees around the house. Those evenings we "shot the breeze," and I would guess that late-night conversations on a windblown porch or patio must have something to do with the origin of that phrase.

That solitary streetlight notwithstanding, the porch was dark, and Grandpa's face, rather like Charlie Marlow's on the *Nellie,* occasionally lit up in a devilish glow when he struck a match to light his pipe or cigar. Like Marlow, "Doc" would tell me stories, not about Africa but about struggling to get by during the Depression, about loading coal cars for the railroad, about his zany neighbor from England who called herself "Queenie," and about the coming of Interstate 70 and the businesses that would close down when Grinnell became at most a gas stop before Oakley to the west or Grainfield, Quinter, or WaKeeney to the east. The shuttered café and broken-down motels along the old highway, which by the 1960s had become a drag strip for bored high school kids, point to the truth of his predictions—but that's another story. This one turns on that streetlight.

Did you ever wonder why boys with BB guns or twenty-twos used to seem to favor streetlights, along with signs, of course, as targets? Did you wonder whether or not it might be because unconsciously they wanted to take back the night, as it were, and reclaim the openness and freedom that night signifies in our culture? It was "Doc" who taught me how to shoot, and I was too cautious and conscious of the hell to pay were I to do something as rash as take down that light. But, as I sat there in the dark with Grandpa, the flicker of the unshielded lamp sometimes caught me full in the eye—and I would think of the rifle. Grandpa didn't much mind the light; it made him feel safe, and I doubt it ever crossed his mind to take it out.

I've had plenty of time to think about lights and rifles over the decades that have intervened since Grandpa passed away and I moved from the country to the city. Along the way, I have had occasion to seal my bond with the night sky—on the deck of a U.S. Navy ship at night in nearly complete darkness, only the muted red safety lights competing with the ineluctable splendor of the stars and, in some cases, with the green phosphorous light emitting from just below the surface of the sea; in the high country in Colorado's Gore Range or Wyoming's Wind River Range, where darkness is made visible by the archipelago of stars bequeathing a second light—not lesser—upon the earth. Even Seattle and San Francisco have their dark places—the shores of Lake Washington after nightfall; Golden Gate Park, if you dare, or Woodside and the Pacific coast, where on a clear night the sea reflects the dark light of the sky and where, in the right places, the intermittent splay of foglight seems to complement, not to lacerate, the darkness.

But by and large, under the penumbra of artificial light emitted from streetlamps, playing fields, automobiles, parking-lot lights, and security lights, it's difficult to find an unadulterated spot of night in the city these days. It's time for a John Ruskin for the night sky. Our cities are besmirched and besmeared not with smog and smoke from the mindless proliferation of factory chimneys (although there is that too), but from the mindless proliferation of surplus light originating from an endless archipelago of electricity-guzzling luminaires. The satellite views of the earth are testimony to the loss of dark places, and the light emissions from major urban centers are evidence for what Michel Serres calls the tectonic force of human beings pressing against the earth—and against the sky. As research is beginning to show the harmful effects of bright artificial light, ranging from disrupting the nocturnal patterns of insects, fish, birds, and animals, to inhibiting melatonin production in the human body, organizations such as the International Dark-Sky Association are making efforts to remedy the senseless proliferation of artificial light across the planet. Nonetheless, cities are slow to respond to the call for more responsible management of light pollution.

My home city of Albuquerque, New Mexico, is a case in point. I live adjacent to a grocery store, now owned by a company that will go unnamed. In December 1999, the Furr's Corporation, which then leased the building, remodeled and expanded the quaint neighborhood store that had once occupied the space. As part of the remodeling, the company installed twelve thirty-foot light poles, each holding two drop-lens fixtures with 1000-watt metal halide luminaires. Our once relatively dark neighborhood was lit up like a baseball park. The so-called Environmental Planning Commission of the City of Albuquerque had approved the design for the remodeling, including the external lighting, even though the lighting configuration turned out to violate the city's outmoded code, and so the store management would not respond to my desperate appeals for some relief from the light trespass extending out into our neighborhood and directly in my backyard. Working with the City of Albuquerque Zoning Department, I affirmed that the fugitive light from the parking lot exceeded the maximum allowable foot lamberts (a measure of brightness) under the extant zoning code. While my teenage son reminded me that a buddy of his had a brand-new BB gun, in a classic case of displacement I resorted instead to the pen. I wrote a letter to the *Albuquerque Journal,* which caught the attention of KOB-TV Channel 4 news. It was now June. On the morning after the newscast, which included shots of me and two of my neighbors being interviewed in the afternoon, and the news reporter doing her show without need of camera lights at the edge of my yard that night, I awoke to find a crew replacing the 1000-watt bulbs with 400-watt bulbs. A couple of weeks later, shields were installed on the fixtures, and the Furr's maintenance engineer, the zoning officer, and I and my neighbors met to agree that a reasonable compromise had been made.

Unfortunately, the shields still left exposed the tips of the drop-lens globes, and we still got some glare from the parking lot. I'm lucky, because my backyard, which is adjacent to the parking lot, is lined with dense Arizona cypress trees, hardy trees for this arid climate. Nonetheless, on my patio at night, particularly when the warm spring or hot summer breezes picked up, the flickering glare from the tips of those bulbs still stabbed intermittently through the gaps in the branches. When the store changed hands after the Furr's bankruptcy, I appealed to the new management to help us out, especially after their maintenance crews began replacing the 400-watt bulbs with 1000-watt bulbs. Again the city was cooperative, and the new management, to our great relief, at first, installed longer shields that fully covered the globes, effectively making the lights full cut-off, that is, directing the light straight down to the parking lot, where it belongs and where it is needed. To the dismay of myself and my neighbors, the maintenance team fabricated the shields from flimsy, light-gauge aluminum, and in the high winds that we get every spring, many of the shields, no doubt to the distress of anyone in the parking lot at the time, peeled off or were taken down for safety reasons. As I write this essay, we are now back where we were in December of 1999, with the exception that the corporate management of the store promises to do something permanently about the lights—either to replace the extant fixtures with completely new full cut-off lights or to install shields that won't rip away in the first heavy east-canyon wind.

The pen, it turns out, was mightier than the BB gun or the twenty-two, because with a single shot of the pen I took out—though now the final outcome is pending—twenty-four 1000-watt metal halide lightbulbs. Nonetheless, without the cooperation of the present store management and their corporate bosses, we would be helpless to do much of anything, as the Albuquerque light ordinance, weak enough in its own right, and the New Mexico Night Sky Protection Act both allow for the grandfathering of old, neighborhood-unfriendly lights. The Dark Skies initiative launched in 2003 has so far not produced a new, more restrictive and responsible city ordinance, so neighborhood organizations and individual citizens are effectively left to negotiate directly with the car dealerships, grocery chains, industrial parks, and sports arenas—and among their neighbors—to remediate light pollution and light trespass issues in the city.

Bringing up the neighbors leads me to a final reflection, perhaps ironic, if not hypocritical. I confess to my own recent complicity in the reckless diffusion of artificial light. In the past eight weeks, my car has been vandalized and burglarized three times. A rash of such crimes has spread throughout the neighborhoods in my area of the city. A row of Japanese black pines lines my driveway where the car—not a fancy one, a 1996 Honda Civic—is parked. A 175-watt mercury vapor, barn-light-style streetlight diffuses light onto my neighbor's yard and driveway to the west of me, and my neighbor to the east of me has a motion-detector light armed with two 100-watt halogen spotlights above his driveway. Across the street, another neighbor has installed an unshielded halogen porch light (called a wall pack) that automatically goes on at dark and shuts off at first light. My car and truck (a 1988 Toyota) have repeatedly been targeted by the vandals and thieves. After filling out the last police report, I called an electrician, ran conduit over my roof, and installed a motion detector light, which I hope will prevent further break-ins that cost me a hefty deductible.

Have I sold out in the name of security, that word that has enabled so much compromise of our human, civic, and environmental rights? Pretty much so. I put up a 150-watt motion-sensing halogen security light that will go off when someone crosses the end of my driveway or approaches the car or truck from either side. In my defense, I could adduce that at least the light is a single fully contained fixture that allows minimal diffusion into my neighbors' yards or into the street, and I have it set to stay on for only one minute at a time—relying on the scare factor to shoo off the nasty perpetrators of these petty but costly misdemeanors. Nonetheless, now my nights at home are awash in light front and back, and whenever I go out on the front porch, it's not the streetlight poking through the waving branches I have to annoy me, but the full swath of light from my own fixture, which augments the light from the streetlamp, which in turn augments the perpetual porch light across the street, as well as (sometimes) my neighbor's motion lights to the east. I should add that none of these lights much bothers my neighbors, and some of them, except for the few equally offended by the light trespass from the store, think I'm a crackpot for raising these issues at all. So, my security light won't annoy anyone but me, it seems.

I think about what "Doc" might have done. If someone had broken into his car, he might well have put up a security light, and he wouldn't have thought twice about its impact on the neighbors. He also would have slept for a couple of days by the door or window with his twelve-gauge at the ready, and he wouldn't have been contemplating shooting at a light. I don't own a gun, which is probably, my wife affirms, a good thing. Everyone on the block would know where to find me if their lights turned up shattered one morning. So, if I want dark night, I can, I must, at least for a few years more, drive to Chaco Canyon (where the light glow from Albuquerque increasingly impinges upon the night sky) or take to the hills above Jemez Springs or go south to Los Lunas or the Bosque del Apache.

One has to drive far these days to find a true night. Immanuel Kant somewhere says, "Two things fill the soul with ever new and increasing wonder and reverence the oftener the mind dwells upon them—the starry sky above me, and the moral law within me." It's the moral law within me that keeps my finger off the trigger; the starry sky above, well, when I can get it, I see deep. If nothing else, in Wordsworthian fashion, I have those memories, steeped in a deep melancholy, of the sky above Hickam Field, filled with the lights of angels and recently departed souls; but I want my children and grandchildren to feel the wonder of the night sky too—and so I take them to those dark places of the earth where the night can still unfold its mysteries and promise, and do what I can to minimize fugitive light in the city.

ORIGINAL COUNTRY

MARK TREDINNICK

I lived for seven years where you could lie down with the moon.

When she was full she'd slouch across the northern sky and loiter around midnight in my bedroom window. I'd turn off the light and let her fall on me. For three or four nights at a stretch each month, in that house at the edge of a cliff, that is how sleep would come, out of a crow-black sky.

I dreamed well there. I made some books. I made some poems. We made, my girl and I, a marriage, and a couple of moon-bright children. I let a plateau dawn on me.

Katoomba's not far west of Sydney—sixty miles or so—but far enough. You can look out at night across a world of gesturing eucalypts and see the city attenuated and brilliant and diminished in the dark, like light leaking under your bedroom door. I remember how, on our first night in the cottage, we lay down and the silence rang and an utter dark pulled itself about us, as though I'd turned the known world off at the wall with the houselights. Katoomba, like most of this wide and thinly settled continent, but unlike the streets where most of us live along its edges, still does night. And it was the night that brought me in those years in that place closer to heaven than I'm likely to come again.

Many nights I walked out late and looked up, especially in the winter. Across the taut black sky the Milky Way, desire path of so many gods of so many cultures, splayed like a jet stream, near enough, it seemed, to touch. For seven years under that sky, strewn as it was at night with fragments of original time, with pieces of the true creation story sewn wildly across its black field by some mad and profligate original god, I felt part of a dreaming world, part of a plateau that had fallen, that moment, from the selfsame infinite and haunted sky, like a gift. And I came inside, and sometimes the moon and a little of the starlight came with me, to dream. Dreams, like stars and moons and deep, deep sleep, are gifts of the darkness. And I dreamed well in the plateau. I dreamed I'd never leave.

But I've come back down to the city now, and the night has gone; and with her have gone the moon and most of the dreams.

·₊˙

The night is like silence and as easily broken.

·₊˙

It is only where the nights are deeply dark that we can read our legends, contemplate our old and common stories, find our selves in our many mythic houses and remember who we are. We are—nearly everywhere in every age—the Hunter and the Seven Sisters. We are Chiron, the wounded healer. We are the emu and the bear and the scorpion. We are the Big Dipper, Venus, the polestar, the northern lights, the southern aurora. Where I live, one is, in particular, the Southern Cross. We are light that takes a hundred generations to arrive. We are suns and stars that may, for all we know, have died centuries ago but whose light still reaches us. Mankind has looked to the sky at night since about the beginning; he has found there patterns and stories that explain to him not only where he is and where he should go, but who he is and how small and yet how divine under so much heaven. The night sky is where one fathoms, among other things, one's self.

We're going to need the night, then, and we're going to need it dark, if we're to remember how we go, each of us and all of us, and if we're to notice the eternity of time and space we belong to. Night puts everything in perspective. Where night is diminished, perspective—humility, humor, generosity, spirit—is lost. Life on earth, which we really conduct in an almost endless universe, loses its eternal context when the rest of the universe eludes us; one's life grows mundane; one grows diurnal, myopic, solipsistic. We need the company of stars to remind us that each breath, each step, each phrase we make, each deal we do, each sparrow's fall, each birth and death, each love we find and keep and lose in the end, each enmity we sustain, each fraudulent or holy war we wage matters as much and as little as a single shard of the Milky Way I used to live beneath. Each one, like each day, like each star, is a god, as Emerson thought, a good one or a bad one. But only one.

Night re-creates heaven every twelve hours or so, depending on the earth's tilt and your place upon it. Dim the heavens, and the earth is not nearly so much herself. Nor are we, upon her, as human. We, too, are dimmed.

But no one wants a dark night of the soul anymore. No one even wants a dark night. And you can forget about the soul.

·₊˙

The night knows things about ourselves that we don't know ourselves.

·₊˙

By day from the balcony of this old house, which is my new home, I can see west as far as the humble dark contour of the plateau. By night I look out north and west across the old suburbs that are the city's tattered selvedge. I cannot see the plateau at night; it casts no light. I look out through the low-voltage glare of the stevedoring yards and the Anzac Bridge to the streetlights of Rozelle and Lilyfield and Annandale; to traffic lights and factory lights and headlamps on moving cars and desklamps in bedroom windows and garden lights and floodlights, where roadworks and rail repairs go on late, to floodlights at parks, where men and women play touch football and night cricket and schoolchildren train for athletics and soccer and basket-ball and parents like me walk their toddlers to sleep; and I look out through the incandescent aura of the city, which lies across a narrow inlet of the harbor just here and whose office blocks stay lighted all night, to where I cannot see the plateau. I look up at a sky gone pale, at a heaven from which most of the angels have fallen.

Cities are factories for unmaking the night. And the world is fill-ing up with cities. Light is what they manufacture. Light, the neces-sary condition for commerce, for traffic of one kind and another, for gossip and learning and labor and games, for the false sense of secu-rity upon which all urban mischief and urbane elucidation depend. For we need light to read by; but learning is an accident of cities, a by-product of wealth and leisure. It is consumption that makes cities go, and consumption thrives on light. The less darkness there is, the more time and inclination and opportunity there are to spend. Consumption is diurnal, but it never wants to stop. So it's learned the trick of eclipsing darkness, denying it and pushing it back, where it can, to make room for itself. But how can you dream when the darkness is too shallow to sink into, the stars too dim to hear.

Cities manufacture lite. Cities put out the sky; they untell our stories; they shallow our dreams; they erase our pasts; they dim our common inheritance; they dismantle our memories; they consume the earth to illuminate the present; they forestall the inevitable; they foreshorten eternity.

And I am living in one right now and loving it, most of the time. Particularly by day. But I miss the night; I hunger for the dark; I wonder nightly what's become of the Milky Way. The moon, too, is much less vivid, and I no longer wax with her and wane. Life goes by in the city like a television drama. It is linear and episodic. A succes-sion of days; and then the repeats. It does not go in circles as the pla-teau did; it does not have the amplitude of life in a place over which the sky still arcs so big and clear.

I am here because work is here and schools and libraries and all the things that make—and thrive in—the light. But what counts most counts for little here: starlight, for instance, and topography and silence. I am here, along with these four million others, because of the city's centripetal pull. Cities are not black holes; they are brilliant white ones, which swallow whole galaxies and lives and legends and histories and out of them make the superabundant present tense in which we live our lives here. Because we feel we must; because we can't resist. And if we dream here, it's either of light or of leaving.

· ₊ *

And you can forget about the soul.

· ₊ *

The night is our original country.

It belongs to all of us equally; and we belong to it. It has no borders or nations. We all travel there without passports much of our lives; we sleep a third of our lives away.

Darkness is where it all began and where it's going to end. For each of us, I mean, and for the whole incredible cosmological miracle of this spinning planet and its confreres. It is the country out of which you came and into which you will return, and into which each night you are, if you're lucky, restored, along with every other waking thing, just so you don't forget the way back.

Darkness is the original country, and it is alive with stories. They are the same stories the whole world over. And sometimes at night they find us.

The other day—one of these city days I lead now, sometimes deep into the night—I wandered, before class, into the university's museum and found myself among the beautiful artifacts of death. "The goal of every Egyptian was to enjoy a long and happy afterlife," I read. That's *after*life. What lay beyond the mortal span was what it was all about. That's a notion hard to find the beauty in, let alone the sense, these days, at least where I come from. I want each day and night to matter for itself, not just as some kind of preparation.

But I've scarcely seen a lovelier thing than that sarcophagus, an animate kaleidoscope of sky and desert, of beetle and ibis and handi-craft; and I've scarcely seen a sadder one than that small casket, made for a seven-year-old boy.

By day, Egyptians believed that the *ba*—that which is super-natural, which is everyone and all time, in each of us—left the body to enjoy the light and air and freedom of the world. But at night the *ba* returned to one's body so that together, body and soul in the body of the night, they might be returned to their original country.

I like a faith that believes in the body, dead and alive. I like a faith that believes in the night. Absent the night, and our soul will have no reason to come home to us.

What if sleep is a rehearsal for such a long afterlife; what if the <u>ba</u> returns to us at night and wants to wander in our sleeping bodies into dreams; and what if it is too light for dreams to find us; what if the night is so diminished we and our *ba* can't find it. What will become of us then?

That's what I found myself standing there wondering beside the body of the seven-year-old boy from Thebes, who lay bound in strips of cloth dark with two thousand years. We know he was seven be-cause someone unwound him and noticed that he still had his baby teeth. And wound him back up again. His name was Horus. I don't know how we know that, but I hope they turn the lights off here at night.

·.•˙

The night is like silence and as easily broken.

·.•˙

In the city you live in a house, at a desk, in a street, in a tower, on a bed, in a kitchen, in a car, even sometimes along a street among your neighbors; but you don't live under the sky, and you don't sleep un-der heaven. You live with the lights on, and you stop looking up.

·₊˙

I lived for seven years where you could lie down with the moon.

·₊˙

Two years ago, when I still lived in the plateau, I rode for three days with two friends along the river that drains all that country. At the end of the first night, we made camp above the river among the Wild Dog Mountains. We watered the horses and hobbled them, and we made a fire and ate, and then we lay on our swags, each of us soon lost to the others in the dark, and we talked. We watched the stars rise, and later the moon, and we could see each other again. Dave knows his stars and his planets. He pointed them out: Orion, the Southern Cross, Saturn, and some other brilliant constellations.

We were so deep in the cleft the river has made in these mountains over all this time that the stars, when they came, came all the way down from the sky and stood—though never still—at the lip of this valley at whose bottom we lay seeing heaven clearly for the first time, and they gave off their white, their pink, their yellow light so brightly out of the black, black canopy of the sky that the horses cast shadows. Even I, and Jim and Dave cast shadows. And our shadows were the pieces of the earth the starlight fell just short of. And they were shaped just like our selves.

Before I slept, an owl called out, and its mate answered from up the slope behind us. Their calls continued for hours and fell like commas between the phrases of my sleep. Five or six times I woke to their *oogh-oogh, oogh-oogh.* Or I woke to the sound of the horses' hobbles, or I woke to the light the stars were singing down. Every time I woke, I was looking at a different sky, for the stars had moved a few bars on.

When the moon got up, I woke to it, too. And each time I woke, the moon had traveled a few degrees more, until it was gone into the west. Before it was light, I watched a shoal of cloud come in from the southeast, chasing the moon, drowning the failing stars. And when the morning came, the sky was gray. Only then did the earth on which I lay stand still. Only then did the sky go quiet, and a light wind came down off the mountains to the river.

·₊˙

Night is when most of creation gets about its works and days.

·₊˙

Lately, I have been dreaming of wolves. And children.

But I have to leave home to dream. I have to go to places where I am alone and where the sky is dark enough for me to hear in my sleep the note each star cries out.

Back in December by Cradle Mountain, I walked home late from dinner with a new friend. We'd eaten in her kitchen, in her old timber shack, by the light of a gas lamp, while outside the rain fell hard and the creek rose. Cradle Mountain, in Tasmania, is a long way from anywhere bright, and it was midnight and there was no moon and rain fell and fell. So I walked home in the darkness with my friend's light strapped to my head. It helped me work out what was path and what was wombat. But it also blinded me, that beam, to most of the small world I was walking in, everything behind and above and to each side. It made the darkness huge around me until I felt I was about to be mugged by it.

So, halfway home I switched off the light. I liked it better that way, but I've got to say I was shocked by how little I could make out in that old-fashioned kind of darkness. I listened better, of course, and heard a whole lot more wombat cough and owl call and pademelon scuttle than I had before I switched the darkness on. But I realized then how diurnal one is—as a traveler, anyway. At night, one is blind. And blindness doesn't work for everything. Such as walking. Nights are for slowness and for being at home. Nights are for other beings, which is why we humans need them so much.

In Australia, for instance, if you've been sleeping, you've missed about 75 percent of the wildlife. Even in these overlit days that's true, even to some degree in the city. And it's somehow good to know that night is when most of creation gets about its works and days.

I went to bed that night with a strange sense that I had left a child outside in the rain. I woke once to coughing, which in my sleep I associated with the child, but which was the wombat beneath the hut. Later I dreamed of Maree, my wife, at home with three children, the youngest a baby. The dream woke me. We had then just two children, but I had this feeling, even on waking, I had forgotten one. I walked outside and the night had cleared. It was 3:00 AM and bright with stars. A black sky was dense with them. It occurred to me that the child I was sensing was one we lost a few years ago, when Maree miscarried, before the two boys came along. When I went back inside I dreamed again. This time I took refuge from weather in a cave with my younger boy, Daniel. He was wandering loudly about, and we were laughing. Then I saw the wolf curled up asleep, and I realized we were in terrible danger. The wolf woke, bared his teeth and came at us. Somehow I held my child away from the animal with one arm, fended off the wolf with the other, and bargained with him for our lives. And he let us go. Or the dream ended with all our lives intact.

The other dream I had about a wolf I had in a room in a house on a dark street on the outskirts of Eugene, Oregon, six months earlier. Alone again. In that dream, a snow leopard came my way along a trail and changed into a wolf. She passed me before she saw me. Then, too, I held my nerve and we faced off, and she left.

The animals, you see, are awake at night. It is their world. Sometimes they come to us in our dreams, and sometimes they are children.

I don't know what these dreams mean. But I think the night does. And I think one day I'll learn.

At night we are afraid; at night we are woken sometimes to who we are and who we have been and who we might be yet. Night delivers intimations of self, messages in forms much less exact than an idea, and more memorable. In parables and poems. In darkness.

A week after dreaming the child and the wolf at Cradle Mountain, I landed back in the city, and Maree told me she was pregnant. With child. She'd found out a week ago, she said.

The night knows things that we don't know ourselves. Yet. Sometimes it tells us darkly what they are. But only when the lights are out.

·₊˙

Darkness is the original country, and it is alive with stories.

NIGHT IN MIND

WILLIAM L. FOX

When I was fourteen I built a telescope and would set the alarm clock to wake me after midnight in order to observe the planets, glowing clouds of gas near Orion's belt, and the barely defined spirals of far-off galaxies. The telescope would be waiting for me in the garage, where it had been cooling down along with the night air to prevent the optics distorting when I wheeled it outside. The Nevada air is so arid that temperatures dive precipitously after sunset. Had I kept the instrument inside the house, I would have had to wait hours for the optics to settle down.

In the mid-1960s the lights of Reno were dim enough that I could see the Milky Way from our front door. When I turned off the living room lights, I felt as if I could step into outer space by simply crossing the threshold. I'd push the ten-inch reflector out onto the front lawn, taking care not to jar the mirror I'd helped grind at the local planetarium. Then I'd align its mount with the polestar and begin to track the objects of my attention. Standing on a stepladder in order to reach the eyepiece, I'd sketch the Great Red Spot as it moved across the face of Jupiter, the changing seasons on Mars, the slow tilt of Saturn's rings.

The first few times I took my scope outside at two in the morning, the police cruising the neighborhood would deliberately blind me with their spotlight. It was a way of immobilizing a kid out after the midnight curfew. I showed them the blurry ice cap at the south pole of Mars, moons revolving around Jupiter, whatever was available that night. They learned to turn off their headlights as they neared the house, and would roll up the circular driveway to take a look for themselves.

My telescopic relationship with the cops came in handy when, a couple of years later in high school, I'd be cruising Reno's main drag on Friday nights, the neon on the casinos so bright it made Virginia Street look like a dance floor. When pulled over for a routine check of the car for beer bottles and other contraband, they recognized me and assumed that I wouldn't be out too late—I'd be busy with my observations. They had no idea how hard-won had been my battle with fear of the night.

When I was three and living in the hills above San Diego, I had nightmares about aliens in spacesuits invading our house. The dreams were so severe my parents thought about sedating me with their own sleeping pills. The first night I spent outside on a camping trip, when I was eight, I spent most of it shivering more from fright than cold. I didn't learn to like the night until I began to look at the stars when I was twelve. By then my parents had divorced, my mother and I had moved to Reno, and she had remarried. For my birthday that year my father, an engineer who was then working with the Deep Space Network at the Jet Propulsion Laboratory in Pasadena, sent me his own telescope, a handsome three-inch refractor in a long wooden case.

Father had been as remote from me as the planets for most of my childhood, but once, almost before I could walk, he lifted me up to that slender instrument so I could view the moon. Its cold mountains stood out on the lunar limb, and the bright empty plains of dust pockmarked by craters hurt my eyes. I cried, demanding to be put down. When older, I asked him when we could look again, but the moment had passed. It was shortly after my parents divorced, when I was ten, that he went to work at JPL collecting signals from spacecraft flying by Venus and the moon. The gift of his telescope was tantamount to an invitation to join him, if not physically then at least intellectually, and I later fitted it to my larger instrument as a finder scope.

Nineteen sixty-two, that year when I turned twelve, was one in which the entire country changed profoundly its relationship with the night sky, with dark, with space. In January John Glenn became the first American to orbit the Earth. *Mariner 2* flew by Venus, *Ranger 4* managed to reach the Moon—and President Kennedy announced a program to follow up with humans. We had begun to explore the solar system, and all across the country people went outside their houses in the evenings to catch a glimpse of one of the spacecraft flying east overhead. Night seemed a new frontier, and my father was part of the effort.

In my early twenties and shortly before my father died, I took up mountaineering. Spending the night outside, often alone, slowly became more than a necessity, rather, a welcome habit. There were years when I seemed to spend more time in a sleeping bag than a bed, and whenever possible I slept in the open in order to see the stars. I came to equate the night with both wisdom and desert. Wisdom because it was where my father had worked, in the perpetual night of space. And desert because its vast sterility—part of what had scared me originally about the moon—was interrupted only by oases of life, or so I assumed then and still do today. I was also then and remain an atheist, but it was easy for me to see how one could long for a father in the sky, and how the world's monotheisms would have grown out of the great sandy deserts. When deprived of the night, I feel as if an essential part of my intelligence about the universe is missing.

And there are times when I have been displaced, literally, from the night. As I write this I have lived for 20,560 days, but have had only 20,455 nights during my fifty-six years and four months. The first time I lost night was for a week in Norway during the summer of 1967. The sun slipped behind the mountains in Bergen, but it never fully set and the stars remained hidden. I would snuggle under a down comforter at midnight after a long day of walking—and just as I started to wonder whether or not the lack of darkness would prevent me from falling asleep, I awoke with a start just in time for breakfast.

I missed nights while working during the summers of 2002 and 2003 in the Canadian High Arctic. Devon Island, the world's largest uninhabited island, sits only nine hundred miles from the North Pole. It's been glaciated so often that it is relatively sterile, its surface a dendritic maze of meltwater channels. In its center is a 38-million-year-old crater where an asteroidal body hit the planet and left a hole twelve miles wide and a thousand feet deep. This is as good an analog environment for Mars as we have, and it's where the National Aeronautics and Space Administration practices going to the Red Planet with live humans. The camp of the NASA Haughton-Mars Project is on the outer rim of the crater, and during the four weeks of summer each year the sun dips down only briefly behind the hills to the west for an hour or two. You're just barely in the shadow of Earth, and it helps to cover your eyes with a bandanna in order to sleep.

How ironic, that we would practice living and working on Mars when we couldn't even see the night sky. And now my Inuit friends in the town nearest to Devon Island, Resolute Bay, are saying that the Arctic night itself is no longer as dark as it used to be. No one believed them until the local meteorologist discovered that a layer of the Arctic atmosphere, recently warmed by global climate changes, was reflecting sunlight from far below the horizon. Even the polar night, the longest and most pure form of that black isotropy we find on earth, is threatened by the ubiquitous footprint of our species.

But the place where I have missed the most nights is in the Antarctic. I spent eleven weeks of the austral summer there in

2001–2, working to understand how humans perceive the largest desert on our world, a place the size of the United States and Canada combined, and where the annual precipitation is about that of the Mojave Desert. It is a continent that has only one sunrise and sunset a year, one day and one night.

I never saw the stars while in the Antarctic, although I visited astrophysicists at the South Pole who were making pictures of the early universe. They weren't using telescopes to look at visible light, so a dark sky wasn't required, but were collecting data from wavelengths farther out in the electromagnetic spectrum. They used an array of instruments cooled as close to absolute zero as they could get. Thermal interference—heat from the horizon, for example—was more bothersome than light and to be eliminated whenever possible; hence the cold at the Pole was more important than dark. But, after months of Antarctic glare I longed for darkness. I would have gladly spent the mandatory six months in order to winter over at the Pole so I could have seen the stars from there during the longest night on earth.

When I left the Antarctic on a military cargo plane bound for New Zealand, I fell asleep along with the forty or fifty other people coming off the ice that day. I woke in midflight gripped with anxiety and couldn't figure out why. I looked out the window and it was dark. My first thought was that we were flying into an enormous storm, that being the only time the sky dimmed on the ice. But no, it was night. Just night. I stared out into the lovely dark, the only person awake on the plane besides the flight crew. A single unblinking light stood off the starboard wing. I went back to sleep.

I spend most of my time writing about how we interact with deserts. People ask me of what value is a place that looks the same in all directions, and I reply that it is there where we can most clearly see the shape of our own minds. I travel with artists and scientists as they image the great open places still in front of us, which in my lifetime have increasingly been reduced to only the most difficult environments. I look at the pictures and maps my fellow travelers produce, and it seems to me that the American landscape photographer Robert Adams had it exactly correct when, in his 1989 book *To Make It Home,* he wrote: "To the extent that life seems a process in which everything is taken away, minimal landscapes are places where we live out with greater than usual awareness our search for an exception for what is not taken away."

Night, by virtue of making apparent "outer space," is both our most minimal and maximal place, and is where and when we inhabit the deepest shape of our mind. Borges noted in his essay "A New Refutation of Time" (1946) that night "suppresses idle details, just as our memory does." I know of no other place to find our deepest mind than in the night, in the great desert all about us that becomes visible as we pass into shadow and the stars appear to define for us its depth. My fear is not of the night anymore, but of losing it, because then we would have no way to know our place.

I live in Los Angeles now, the lights of which are so extensive that it is difficult to see any celestial evidence save the brightest stars. During the riots of 1992, when the power went out, residents called their local police stations to ask what was wrong with the sky: there was something long and white floating overhead. It was the Milky Way, which they had never before seen. That great road in the sky had been replaced by the grid of streetlights in a city where the police never turned off their lights.

I no longer have a telescope, but when driving through the desert at night I often pull out the binoculars. I'll stop, brace myself with elbows on the roof, and look around at whatever I can see. Most often I spend my time looking past the edges of the Milky Way, where the rim of our galaxy falls away and truly deep space becomes evident. Falling upward is the sensation I first had when looking through my father's telescope. It is still the pull I feel, looking for what remains when all else is removed by the night.

PART FIVE

OUR ANIMAL BODY

Sleep cycles, fear, giving birth and caring for our young, reliance on the earth's body for our own body's sustenance—we share much with our animal neighbors. In this section, six writers explore natural cycles in which darkness is vital. In "Nightfall," biologist Robin Wall Kimmerer's portrait of the earth at "twilight, that long blue moment," we read of how our bodies, like those of the plants, animals, and birds around us, "all live by the exhalations of the plants," which in turn rely on the natural rhythm of light and dark. Christina Robertson follows with "Circadian Heart," showing the serious consequences to animals denied the regular sustenance of darkness. Having to feel her way down a mountain trail in darkness, Janisse Ray feels in "Against Eternal Day" an affinity for those animals "wired to move in darkness" and wonders "might we humans too be made confused by absence of darkness?" The value of fear is James Bremner's topic in "Fear of the Night." He wonders how children who never face their fear of the dark are to learn courage. Scott Russell Sanders, in an excerpt from his essay "Earth's Body," faces his fear—of mortality—by walking out into the darkness of his backyard at night. And, in "Heart of the Sky," Jennifer H. Westerman writes of becoming a mother for the first time and wondering if her daughter will know the night as she has.

NIGHTFALL

ROBIN WALL KIMMERER

Across the valley, over the great expanse of forest, the sunset light flares orange against a far-off window and it flickers like a distant fire. Atop this high, wild ridge, the last rays of the day gild the spires of spruce. Shadows open wells of darkness among the treetops. The revolution of the earth turns us away from the sun, carrying these mountains into the night. Golden glow to the west, pregnant silver glow of moonrise to the east, and arched between them the radiant dome of deep blue twilight. A wood thrush calls from the shadows and echoes over the valley, a glittering silvery decoration hung on the branches of dusk.

All the long, hot afternoon, the light has traveled across 93 million miles of dark and empty space. The planet basks like a turtle on a log afloat in the celestial sea, soaking up the light. And all the forest responds; leaves rise, petals open, water courses up the trunks of trees and departs as vapor to mingle with the clouds.

Sun warms the bare dome of granite. Rocks expanding in the heat, the whole mountain arches its back, stretching in the sun. The swell of the granite is just enough to fracture a crust of lichen that clings there. The gathering heat drives off the moisture from a tuft of moss, and one by one the leaves shrivel, moving slowly to spiral round the stem. The whole motion of the mountain is light made animate. And animated by light.

In the noonday brilliance, hot air rises off the summit and spirals upward in powerful gyres invisible but for the redtail riding the thermals. The updraft pulls a breeze along the surface that sets the treetops waving and ruffles the petals of anemones in the clearing. Each blossom, a bowl of white petals, rotates on its stem to follow the sun. Even the tree leaves follow the sun, turning their broad planes to track the path of the sun across the sky. Light penetrates the epidermis of the leaf, where deep within the leaf cells the chloroplasts, too, are tied to the movement of the sun. They migrate across the cytoplasm to the bright side of the cell and gracefully turn their long flanks to meet the incoming sun.

Light sets the chlorophyll to vibrating, starts electrons spinning, whirring turbines for the transformation of light and air into sugar. The fires of photosynthesis are stoked by the intake of carbon dioxide. Every leaf, every pine needle, every blade of grass is dotted with stomata, tiny pores in the leaf, microscopic portals to the inner labyrinth of the leaf. There may be as many as one hundred stomates in just one square centimeter of leaf. At the scale of the bumblebee's foot, resting on a leaf, the pores look like open eyes, watching. Each is an open circle, bordered by two crescent-shaped guard cells, like a heavy-lidded eye, squinting into the sun. Through every pore, an inhalation of carbon dioxide and an exhalation of oxygen. This is the fundamental chemistry of the forest, the reciprocity between all living beings. Redtail, bee, fox, and child all live by the exhalations of the plants. And in turn, animals breathe out the carbon dioxide that plants breathe in, a perpetual cycle of mutual responsibility. Breathing alone keeps the world in balance. Oblivious to the source of their very breath, at the house down in the valley, the grass gets mowed and the kids run laughing in a game of tag until they fall, laughing breathlessly in the grass.

But now, as our side of the earth turns away from the light and the sun disappears below the bright line of the horizon, everything changes. Twilight, that long blue moment, hung on the cusp of night and day, poised between sunset and moonrise. The mountain seems to hold its breath, waiting to exhale. On the edge of yin and the edge of yang, the energy of the earth is palpable. Never does the earth feel more alive than at the moment when she takes a last deep breath of day, and the night arrives on her sigh.

With nightfall, the very air is changed and the direction of energy flow between earth and sky reverses its direction. By day, the sun-warmed air spiraled upward. Without the sun to feed its ascent, the air that rose beneath the redtail's wings suddenly cools and the hawk sinks like a stone and lands in the shadowy canopy with a clumsy flapping of wings.

The cooling air settles onto the land. You can feel its weight on your skin and smell its sweet damp. There is that moment of cool skin, and a little shiver lets you know that the equilibrium has begun to shift. What was rising now is falling. The fallen air begins to move, a gentle avalanche of air. It slides downslope, hugging the contours, filling the low places like an invisible river. Heavy with its own weight the air comes flowing down the hill. It passes by like a wall of cool that leaves the hairs standing up on your arms.

Cool air cannot hold as much moisture as warm air and must lay its burden down. What was taken now is given back. Cool air flowing over warm rock lays a sheen of dew on the skin of the earth. The water taken by the sun is now returned as dewdrops to the leaves of moss. And one by one, the crinkled leaves unfold. Beads of moisture cling to the furry back of the bumblebee. The slide of cold air from the mountain spawns a diaphanous fog among the treetops. Moisture condenses on the feathery branches of the hemlocks and, drop by silvery drop, falls to the ground.

Deep in the trunks of trees, the day's water is held high aboveground in capillary tubes of wood, pulled upward by the sun. As the light goes, the motive force of evaporation is quelled and the tension that holds the columns of water is released, yielding to gravity. The upward current now flows backward, and the soil around each tiny root becomes black with moisture. Nightfall gives back what the day has taken.

And yet, nightfall is the time when the children are called inside and the doors are closed. How will they know the way of the world? The give and take of it? The fathers go through the house and shut the windows against the cool river of air draining off the mountains. As the dark falls, the lights are turned on, creating an anti-night so thorough they blind themselves to the coming of the stars. It is there for the taking, every evening of every day, a wonder.

A sleeping child, a sleeping mountain. Everything slows down in sleep, the core temperature drops, the heartbeat, the breath, the brain. Even the brain waves slow and relax into long, low-frequency signatures of serenity. Only the eyes flicker, with rapid eye movement of dreaming, of memories retrieved. It is the same for the land. The breezes drop, the stones begin to cool, and the fox slips in and out of shadow like a dream.

The sun's warmth lingers for a time in the granite, but eventually the mountain, a sink for heat during the day, becomes at night a source. The energy flow is reversed, where heat flows not from sky to rock, but from rock to sky. The rocks send the memory of sunlight reradiating back into space from whence it came. The day's heat is gradually released like a woodstove slowly cooling when the fire goes out. Solar energy comes to the world as an allegro of short, high-energy wavelengths, but leaves the world as an adagio by moonlight in the slow, graceful wavelengths of infrared, the resting brain waves of a sleeping mountain.

As it gives up its heat, the dome of the rock contracts again. The edges of the fissured lichen meet once more. The whole mountain moves like the slowly rising and falling chest of a sleeper.

As the land falls into darkness, the open eyes of the stomates grow heavy and begin to close. The very breath of the forest is changed with the coming of night. The land is a producer of oxygen by day, a consumer by night. Darkness pulls the plug on the engines of photosynthesis, which sputter to a halt. Unused carbon dioxide pools around the leaves. All night long, a myriad of beings, the ferns, the trees, the prowling lynx, the firefly, the white-capped mushroom gleaming in the moonlight—all breathe in the day's stockpile of oxygen. And breathe out carbon dioxide. Through the course of the night, oxygen levels in the woods decline, while the CO_2 rises, with the collective exhalations of the forest, the sleep breathing of the land.

The air lies close to the earth at night. Gone are the rising updrafts, the breezes. A thick blanket of air rests upon the forest floor, where the air mingles closely with the breath of humus, the fragrance of a mossy log. Into that stillness, mushrooms rise and spread their gills. Shelves of fungi along the log ready themselves. Spores release in a cloud of nocturnal plankton, drifting like a dream, carrying the rich sweet fragrance of the night.

As plant eyes close, others open. Owls blink and stretch their wings. Fox, bat, skunk, and vole emerge into the welcoming darkness.

Lights twinkle in the valley below. The blue light of television flickers behind the windows. They sit and breathe the same stale air, while without notice the moon rises over the mountains, draping the world in its own blue radiance.

CIRCADIAN HEART

CHRISTINA ROBERTSON

One April night on the shore of a threatened freshwater lake in the middle of Nevada I held a common loon in my hands. Its webbed feet were hot. The loon struggled. Mike, the wildlife biologist taking a blood sample, told me, "You've got to hold on tight."

A second biologist held the loon's head. Against my spread palms I felt the bird's heart beat, fast and hard. I'd held birds before, mostly small, always dead—a downy woodpecker, a tanager, a meadowlark, a hummingbird—but never a seventeen-pound loon frantic to free itself. My animal heart beat hard in reply.

Our midnight flotilla, ornithologists, biologists, and volunteers armed with flashlights and nets, had captured this loon and five others to assess their health. A stiff chop cut across the lake that night, muffling the loons' calls, hiding them between swells. The first hour we hunted in circles, seeing and hearing only wind on water. Red-eyed birds, loons see well underwater and at night. When finally we spotted a few of the hundred-odd loons counted earlier on the lake, we'd used the flashlights to approach and daze them long enough to scoop them into our waiting nets.

Now, in my shaking hands, the loon's chest heaved. Its feathers felt oily and dense and soft, softer even than fur. The bird opened its bill. The biologist filled a syringe with blood, then one more. A deep red drop beaded on the white belly of the loon. It opened its bill, forcing a weak tremolo call. "Bird's too stressed. Time to finish up," Mike said.

On cue I let go of the loon. It was whisked into a cage for the night. In the morning a tiny transmitter would be surgically implanted in the loon's back. If the bird lived and continued migrating north, a signal would be picked up by satellite telemetry, letting biologists track this loon to its summer breeding waters.

Still shaking, my empty palms shone with oil. They would smell like fish for days.

Out on the lake under a waning moon and the constellation Taurus, other loons were staging. Mostly solitary, during spring and fall migrations loons flock together to feed, stake out territory, and, with luck, find a mate. A nocturnal chorus began. Yodeled notes echoed in long, reedy strings across the water, male loons singing their territories. My husband, John, and I—spring newlyweds—climbed into sleeping bags and listened, too amped on adrenaline to sleep.

.₊˙

Accounts of spring migration date back three thousand years. Circa 335–326 BC, in his *History of Animals,* Aristotle records cranes migrating from the Scythian steppes to the marshes of the Nile. In the book of Jeremiah the instinctual wisdom of migrating birds is contrasted with wayward humanity: "Even the stork in the heavens knows its times; and the turtledove, swallow, and crane observe the time of their coming; but my people do not know the ordinance of the Lord" (8:7). Migration, here, is an ordinance, a holy law of the body tied to the seasonal round, the tilt of the earth as it orbits the sun. "To everything there is a season . . ." reads the book of Ecclesiastes in the Old Testament. The seasonal wheel codified in twelfth-century almanacs predicting tides, eclipses, and weather still shapes how we experience the passage of time.

Likewise, just as the earth spins one full turn on its axis every twenty-four hours, all life follows cycles of darkness and light. A circadian clock binds the rhythms and habits of each plant and animal to the amount of light in the sky. Butterflies and bees pollinate morning glories. Moths pollinate moonflowers. (Just this morning I freed a small, dun-colored moth—what need have moths for a butterfly's palette?—from a thick spider's web. The moth flew off, in search of the dark.)

Wolves hunt at night, humans by day. Moose, deer, and antelope, all foragers, emerge from hiding in the liminal hours of dusk and dawn. Common nighthawks take wing at twilight to feed on clouds of newly hatched moths. Once, driving through a high-desert dusk near the Owyhee River, John and I watched as dozens of nighthawks appeared in the sky as if rising from sagebrush, swooping and darting through motes of pink, mothy air.

Like songbirds, like nighthawks, like the loon with the base flute in its throat, like crickets and owls and soft-bodied bats, our human bodies are hardwired to circadian rhythms.

.*

Not strictly nocturnal *Gavia immer,* the common loon, sleeps at night floating out on deep water, its head tucked into its feathers. In the aeon before electricity (ABE), humans slept when darkness fell and rose at daybreak. Like *Gavia immer,* the species *Homo sapiens* belongs to the kingdom Animalia. *Animalia,* Latin for "animals," comes from *anima,* meaning "breath" or "life force," or "soul." Many people who view the human being as the lone possessor of a soul distance themselves from their animal origins. Why consider the source of our breath? Does it matter if we lose track of our connection to other species? Must we ask who we are in relation to the loon asleep on the lake?

Considering our era of lost wilderness—diminishing wild lands, the "oil-soaked otter"—Gary Snyder asks, "Where do we start to resolve the dichotomy of the civilized and the wild?" We walk upright, we use language, we think in abstractions, we use tools. Yet as Snyder says, "Our bodies are wild."

Cell by cell, breath by breath, what sustains us mammal primates is water, air, blood, food, sex, hormones, and sleep.

Take the link between sleep and the hormone melatonin, for instance. Secreted at night by the pituitary gland, melatonin works as an antioxidant and keeps estrogen and testosterone levels in check. Dr. David Blask, a leader in the field of neuroendocrinology, calls melatonin "the hormonal expression of darkness." According to Dr. Stephen Pauley, moderator of the 2001 International Dark Sky Association panel "The Physiological and Pathological Effects of Exposure to Light at Night on Humans," Blask's ongoing research suggests a strong link between decreased levels of melatonin and an increased risk of breast and ovarian cancers. Pauley explains that in an experiment designed to measure the effects of nighttime exposure to light, Blask "implanted a known strain of breast cancer cells (MCF-7) into the groins of rats." In such experiments, Pauley notes, "rat blood vessels [soon] grow into the cancer cells and provide a nourishing medium for cancer cell growth and from which blood samples may be taken." Blask then split the rats into two groups. One group was not exposed to any nighttime light. The other group was exposed to light "at luminosities as low as .02 foot candles" placed three feet away from their cages. Subsequent blood tests were conclusive. The rats kept in the dark, Pauley reports, experienced a natural nocturnal spike in melatonin and a slow growth in cancerous cells. In the light-exposed rats, melatonin levels fell and the cancer cells "grew rapidly."

Blask's research reveals the natural clockwork in our circadian rhythms. When we expose ourselves to artificial light at night, we disrupt our body's production of melatonin, our estrogen levels spike, and we leave our immune systems wide open for free-radical cells to run amok. Blask notes that several studies show breast cancer rates among blind women are 40 percent lower than among sighted women. In developing countries the rate of female breast cancer is one in thirty-five. In the industrialized—that is, lit-up—world, one woman in seven will contract breast cancer. Underscoring Blask's research is the fact that among female graveyard-shift workers breast cancer rates are 50–70 percent higher: two to three women of every seven who work graveyard shifts will get breast cancer.

Of breast cancer's known causes—pollutants, fatty diets, heredity, and, it now appears, exposing ourselves to light at night—dimming the lights could well lessen our risk. Working against our circadian rhythms is draining our bodies of darkness they need to recharge. In denying our animal need for sleep we deny our own mortality. Burning the midnight oil is killing us.

·₊˙

Artificial light is killing wild birds in equally epidemic numbers. Though not nocturnal, most songbirds migrate at night. Small and mid-size birds are easy prey for daytime migrators like hawks, kestrels, and eagles. Dark skies make for safer passage. At night the atmosphere stabilizes, cool temperatures make avian thermoregulation easier, and stars help birds navigate flyways that predate *Homo sapiens*. How did our species' late arrival during the Middle Paleolithic era earn us sway over herons, cranes, and loons that evolved 60 million years ago? Is the starlight ours to obliterate?

By many estimates based on body counts, millions of birds die annually during their spring and fall migrations. In urban areas radio towers and lit buildings kill hundreds of thousands of songbirds—vireos, orioles, waxwings, warblers, tanagers, kinglets, flycatchers—each night during spring migration. Bright and blinking lights draw birds down from the sky toward reflected lights they confuse for stars. In his elegy for roadkilled animals, "Apologia," Barry Lopez asks, "Who are these animals, their lights gone out? What journeys have fallen apart here?"

Years ago on a morning walk with my friend Susan, we found an Anna's hummingbird, intact and warm, on the sidewalk in front of Reno's Porsche building. A drop of blood hung from the tip of its bill. This was late August. The bird would have been migrating; northwestern Nevada sits under a North American flyway. Like so many office towers, the Porsche building is a scape of glass framed by steel: a four-sided, twelve-story mirror. A daylight migrator landing on a stormy night, the hummingbird must've collided with plate glass. Susan bent down and cupped the hummingbird in her palm, stroked its violet throat, felt the tiny break in its neck. "It's so light," she said. "It's like holding air."

We tucked the bird into the vines of her morning glories, periwinkle blooms that would wither by dusk. Resting a finger on its throat one last time, she asked, "Have you ever listened to a hummingbird?"

Back then I hadn't. These days I hear in the whirring, buzzing, amped-up chatter of a hummingbird—whose animal hearts have been known to beat 1,360 times a minute—an avant-garde string quartet. Iridescent flash, hover, dive, sharp chatter, sharp, sharp, buzz. Zig zap, waggle tail, flash, sharp chatter, buzz, loop up, dive, loop up, zip-buzz, zip-buzz gone. It's a music that rattles me, plucks the top off my skull, makes my pulse soar.

·₊˙

Like human beings, songbirds rely on the hormone melatonin for survival. Back in 1999—not long before *The First World Atlas of the Artificial Night Sky Brightness* reported that two-thirds of the world population can no longer see the Milky Way with the naked eye—scientists at Johns Hopkins and the Max Planck Institute proved that melatonin, not testosterone, regulates bird song and mating behavior. As the days grow longer, according to Hopkins psychologist

Gregory Ball, a songbird's high vocal center, or "HVC," found in the brain, balloons from "the size of a pepper flake to a marble." A decrease in melatonin secretions causes the bird's HVC to grow so he can sing longer and louder during mating season.

Come late February I listen to male red-winged blackbirds reclaiming their perches in cattail marshes, singing out hoarse duels that become, as spring waxes, strong and sweet skeins. Near summer's end, as the days grow shorter and the nights longer, melatonin secretions increase, a songbird's HVC gradually shrinks and so does his urge to sing. So while our human need for melatonin is tied to a twenty-four-hour circadian cycle, in songbirds melatonin secretion is seasonal, waning in spring and waxing in autumn.

The red-winged blackbird's instinct to fly south before the fall equinox is an instinct triggered by precise cycles of dark and light. These cycles drive our hormones, change the composition of our blood. Inside the seasonal wheel day follows night, a circle inside a circle, life's circadian heart.

.*

Like many songbirds, members of family Gaviidae, including the common loon, fall mostly silent during winter. Perhaps song would be spendthrift without sex and family life at stake?

The April morning after the loon hunt—an unorthodox honeymoon for John and me—surgery began on the six captive birds. Then the loons would be released, and all of us would wait to discover if these birds died, or lived to finish their spring migration. The transmitted data would be used to help safeguard their habitat.

When the biologist's scalpel sliced through the thick skin of the first loon, a low, slow wail, three stabbing notes, filled the Walker Lake Community Hall. I stepped outside and let John, of stronger stomach, watch for us both.

Gusty spring winds still whipped across the water, scalloping the surface. Sand blew. Larry Neel, the Nevada Division of Wildlife biologist who'd taken me along on a spring bird count of the Carson sink, stood staring out at the Gillis Range on the east side of the lake. "Those loons are taking one for the team," he said.

Hereafter, each of these birds would live with a two-inch antenna protruding from its back. Of course these birds would never breed.

·₊˙

The summer before, camping with John on British Columbia's Slocan Lake, we'd heard a yodeling loon. All night our tent had been wracked by wind and squalls. At dawn the ghostly quavering of a loon roused us from our sleeping bags. His song rippled in waves across still blue gray water.

To hear the riff of a loon for the first time is to taste the pique and marrow of loneliness. You swallow rosy light, time, darkness, all dying. John, who'd never heard a loon before, stood on the beach, a master ventriloquist calling back to the loon. Even though the loon didn't call back, that call is one of the reasons, come April, I married him.

·₊˙

We human beings seek what we imagine are better lives elsewhere, moving for reasons rooted in culture, politics, our own discontent. Common loons, like all migrating birds, respond to ancient cycles of light and heat, cold and dark, flying thousands of miles twice a year to breed and survive. Listen. The flute in the throat of the loon sings the cycles and rhythms, the seasons and days and nights, the blood coursing through our animal hearts. Why not listen to the sky? Come autumn, the loon on the lake will fly south.

AGAINST ETERNAL DAY

JANISSE RAY

One evening when I was a young woman, I was caught on Springer Mountain in Georgia when darkness fell. I had been running for over an hour, trying to beat night to the trailhead, while the pupils of my eyes ever widened to sweep in the last tail feathers of day. But after sundown, and after twilight, and after dusk, a blackness descended that stopped me dead.

The night was moonless. I couldn't see a thing, except when I looked down, my clothing glowed dully, until I appeared even to myself as a ghost. My body had vanished, as had the entire world. I could curl somewhere in the leaves and wait for morning, ten hours hence, or I could attempt to find my way down the long backbone of the mountain. The plummeting temperatures of early spring made my decision.

The path, decades old, was a long groove in the ground. On either side of the trail, the forest floor was covered with leaves that sang and rattled their dryness. Had the trail been more used, it would have been worn down to earth and pebble. But hikers were only beginning to start their treks along the Appalachian Trail, and the path was not kicked clean. Two missteps and I would be lost.

I removed my shoes. My feet hovered, lightly searching the cool earth, and inched ever forward. I went down to hands and knees, feeling for the smooth indentation, feeling the place that was the most cleared of leaf-litter and twigs, making each step a certainty.

Those two miles were at glacial speed; by degrees I kept to the trail.

 ·,·

That night my senses sharpened. As in true blindness, the brain, in the absence of sufficient light, opened capacity once devoted to vision to other sensory receptors. My body was a sponge, highly alert to information transmitted to my brain via my senses. Night vision, after all, is a sense as important as any other, and a skill as helpful as swimming. The human eye has the ability to adjust to darkness, its pupil opening wide to gather any available dusting of light. To have night vision requires good eye health as well as practice navigating darkness, in order to exercise the light-sensitive rod cells of the retina. My eyes began to see.

.·.*

Once when I lived in the Andes Mountains of Colombia, I met a man who had been born in a small village reachable only by foot. He was ten years old, he told me, when he first saw what he called "luz artificial." Artificial light. By day and by night, as he grew into a man, his light came only from fire, natural and real.

All my life I have attempted to be true to night. No flashlights. Streetlamps shielded, disconnected. No night-lights illuminating the bathroom. No door lights during an evening away. I do this not only because throwaway batteries and lights left burning insult my sense of frugality, but because fear is behind most night illumination.

I was the kind of kid who checked every night under my bed and in my closet. I navigated the dark house light switch to light switch. In accepting darkness, then, I have not spared myself terror. I have crept slowly through night, arms raised to protect my eyes. I have entered dark rooms, clawing at air, terrified that I will feel a human face, that I will trip over a human limb. I have memorized numbers of stairs, maps to bathrooms, grids of furniture, gauntlets of flower beds and shrubbery. My desire is to confront fear, to walk even through darkness as if unafraid.

We have been told that day is good, night is evil. Day is productive, night is wasted. Day is for wakefulness, night for sleeping. Day is white, night is black.

And I have judged the quality of a place by its light. So that on the first night when I arrive someplace new, I go outside and look up. The more stars in the sky and the brighter the sash of Milky

Way, the happier I am. I remember a thousand night skies. I remember best the darkest nights. I remember Montana prairie when Hale-Bopp streaked through. I remember the Alaska sky. I remember the Perseids in Nova Scotia, the depth of black velvet in the Sacred Valley of Peru. One autumn night in Mississippi, Mars hovered as close to Earth as it had been in 60,000 years, and another spring evening, us camped on the Altamaha River, five planets—Jupiter, Saturn, Mars, Venus, and Mercury—bunched beneath a boat moon.

What we people miss, in our love for daylight and things of day, is a nocturnal natural history of fabulous proportion. Spring and fall, birds fill the night sky, mostly unseen and unheard. High in the universe yellow-billed cuckoos migrate, their bodies silhouetted against harvest moons. On spring nights, male pinewoods tree frogs hop to the edges of vernal pools, where they call and call, begging a female to come to them. Flatwoods salamanders pick a cold rainy fall night to start their treks downhill to ephemeral ponds to breed.

By night, sea turtles migrate toward sand dunes, where they painstakingly dig nests in which to lay their leathery eggs. Mullet leaping in Gulf waters throw up spumes of phosphorescence. Owls hunt the understory.

These animals are wired to move in darkness. Light will confuse them, make them head in wrong directions, stall them, disorient them.

Might we humans too be made confused by absence of darkness? Might, in eternal artificial light, we fail to thrive? Might constant light be a source of torture?

My friend Sandy West, who lives on an otherwise uninhabited barrier island off the coast of Georgia, talked to me about her sadness for the lives of most young people nowadays. "They will never know total silence or total darkness," she said. "We have all but completely taken night away from them."

Flying over cities at night, looking down, I think, "It might as well be day down there."

What has confused us is the double entendre. Our desire for

meaning keeps us reaching for greater clarity and luminosity. But we confound lucidity with kilowatts. We confuse artificial light with enlightenment.

Therein lies a greater fear: that we humans might be so afraid of darkness that we, for a time, would destroy it, thus banishing the illumination that darkness brings.

·₊·

Every year on cold rainy nights in March and April, spotted salamanders leave hibernation to labor across the littered and cold floors of birch and maple forests, crawling downhill toward freshly thawed ponds and woods pools, where they will breed. Thousands upon thousands pause at the edges of roadways, and then begin to cross.

A few hundred cross Orchard Street, a dirt road near my home at the time in the small city of Brattleboro, Vermont, bent for a cattail pond. On these nights not only do salamanders migrate, but also red newts, woods frogs, toads, and spring peepers.

The salamanders are a wet gray, spotted bright yellow. They are as much as eight inches long. Their eyes are endearing, their bodies fleshy and willing. Some of them are twenty years old.

On these nights I go help the animals across Orchard Street. I have had to obtain a flashlight to do this work. If no one does it, a portion of them are crushed beneath the vehicles that pass, and the carnage is unbearable.

Sometimes when night grows late and the traffic infrequent, I switch off the light. The dark wood collects around me. Though the frog chorus from the pond is deafening, I hear tiny rustlings through leaves and the slight movement of animals passing, headed for water. A barred owl calls. The rain sounds like small and constant kisses. I dare not move, for fear of treading on some life. I stand for a long time beneath night clouds, looking into the inscrutable distance. Life flows and flows past me, like a river, until it finally lifts me up in its insurgence and delivers me to the edge of a luscious and telling obscurity.

FEAR OF THE NIGHT

JAMES BREMNER

I was afraid of the night as a child. There was no reason for my fear. In a tiny village in western Scotland fifty years ago there was nothing to fear: there were no dangerous animals on the entire island of Britain, there were no more than two hundred people within ten miles of my home, every one known personally to me, and in those days people did not imagine kidnappers and molesters hid behind every bush. But there was an excuse for my fear. Rain clouds drifted in from the Atlantic most nights and blotted out the stars, there were no street or porch lights, and every window was heavily draped against the damp chill: the dark was absolute.

As a child my nightly chore was to take the empty milk bottles to the bottom of the driveway and leave them where the milkman could find them first thing in the morning and replace them with full. I loved this chore, for I had a passionate craving for milk all through childhood, and I would have braved any fear to ensure a fresh supply the next morning. Bravery was necessary for me to open the door and step out into the utter blackness. I would stand with my back pressed against the closed door, waiting for my eyes to adjust and hoping that tonight there would be a faint gleam of starlight through a break in the clouds. Soon enough, wet and cold and shame would force me to start down the driveway. It was about one hundred feet to the end, and I remember the dreadful feeling of each slow step taking me farther into the night. The instant the empty milk bottles were safely in position, I turned and fled back to the house, legs pumping and eyes tight shut.

I am glad I was once afraid of the night. Each night for years, I learned how to function despite the fear, which is called courage. Although my fear of the night was irrational, the courage I learned was real and has served me as an adult against the fear of real dangers.

·₊˙

I finally lost the last of my fear of the night in Africa. Hiking through game parks, curled up in a flimsy tent among a horde of rutting hippopotamus, confronting a looming elephant on the narrow path to the latrine at midnight, finding the tracks of a lion the next morning, I was more thrilled than afraid. The fear came one night on hearing steps outside the tent, human footsteps. On that occasion they were probably just ivory poachers, but the rational, genuine fear that they were freedom fighters was so intense, so stark, that it revealed other fears, even my old fear of the dark, to be trivial.

·₊˙

These days, I camp in the Canadian woods where, it is true, bears kill a handful of people each year, but where that rustling in the bushes is most likely just a chipmunk. If it is a bear, I am sure to fear him far less than a lovesick hippopotamus.

I wonder sometimes how modern children, constantly bathed in light, can ever learn courage. They seem to have very few opportunities to practice since they are surrounded at all times with painstaking precaution and have their way lit constantly, day and night. The few children that I know not only seem fearful when confronted with a genuine challenge, such as paddling a dark lake or hiking a trackless forest, but they seem unashamed of their fear. Instead of working to hide their fear and then to overcome it, I think they have been taught to exaggerate so someone will come along to install a night-light, a streetlight, or otherwise remove the cause of the fear so far away that it never need be confronted. Courage, which is no more than the management of fear, must be practiced. For this, children need a widespread, easily obtained, cheap, renewable source of something scary but not actually dangerous. I have this humorous vision of children, in their millions, in cities around the world, pulling up paving stones and digging down into the earth, mining for darkness.

Now, I still don't like cloudy nights, not because they are dark, but just the reverse, for now they are bright. My house has two twenty-foot-high walls of uncurtained glass, oriented so I can watch the sunset in the evening and the northern lights at night. There is a small city fifty miles away, normally hidden behind a hill. On overcast nights, though, the city lights reflect from the clouds and wreck my beautiful view of the night with a sickly artificial glow that gets brighter every year.

FROM "EARTH'S BODY"

SCOTT RUSSELL SANDERS

Seal tight your roof and walls and they will shelter you from weather, but they will not shield you from fear. Fear comes on me now in this twitching hour between midnight and dawn. I cannot say exactly which hour, because I am afraid to look at a clock. My back aches and shoulders throb from splitting a cord of oak, which was a foolish way for a man of forty-six to spend a day in August. Here in southern Indiana, August is a slow oven. The bones bake, the blood thins, the mind oozes into holes.

Even with windows gaping, the house catches no breeze. The only stir of breath comes from my wife, my daughter, my son, and me. Kept awake by the heat or my panicky heart, I tossed for a spell on damp sheets, cooking in my own juice, until dread snatched me out of bed. I put on a loose pair of shorts, all the clothing I could bear, and crept downstairs. Now I huddle in the kitchen, the lights on, tea steeping. I trace the grain in the table—also oak, like the wood I split all day—running my finger along the curved lines as though one of them might lead me out of the pit.

Surely you know the place I am talking about. You have skidded down the slope toward oblivion, for shorter or longer stays. And so you realize the pit is not a gap in something solid, like a hole in rock, but the absence of all solidity, the square root of nowhere and nothing. I go there too often, never willingly, usually dragged from bed by the scruff of my neck.

A dog will bite a rag and shake it, first playfully, then earnestly, and at last furiously, with snarls and bristling hair, as though outraged by the limp cloth. Just so, in the dark hours, certainty of death seizes me by the throat. The grip is hesitant to begin with, a teasing nibble, then the teeth clamp tight and I am lifted and shaken like the flimsiest rag. It is a dance I have known since childhood, this midnight shimmy with dread, and yet each time it sweeps me up my belly churns and muscles jerk as though for the first time. Nothing else in my life—not the tang of blackberries or the perfume of lilacs, not even the smack of love—is so utterly fresh, so utterly convincing, as this fear of annihilation.

Such alarm over the quenching of mind's wavery flame! Is this any way for a grown man to feel? Suitable or not, it is what I do feel. I rehearse this midnight panic because I cannot separate the bright thread of fear from the story I have to tell, which is about making oneself at home on the earth, knowing the earth as one body knows another.

I sip the tea while staring at the kitchen window. The glass gives back the reflection of a balding man with taut lips, shadows in the hollows of cheeks and in gashes beside a crooked nose, black sockets where the eyes should be. No comfort there. The image is thinner and more fragile than the glass on which it hovers. I shift in my chair and the face disappears.

I raise a hand to my cheek, feel the stubble of whiskers, the slick of sweat, the nub of skull. Stubborn, those whiskers. Shaved morning after morning, they are not discouraged. They will persevere after my heart and lungs have quit. I take a dish towel from the drawer, sniff sunlight in the air-dried cloth, and wipe my face. Immediately the sweat begins to bead again, on skin that draws closer each year to the contours of the skull.

If you are older than thirty or so, you have shared this moment. You have studied the cracks in your face, the slump in your belly, the leaching of color from your hair. You have traced erosion under the tips of your fingers and in the icy pools of mirrors. No perception is more commonplace; and no emotion is more futile than fussing about it. Like any tree or hill, like any house heaved up into the weather, our bodies wear down. Inside the furrowing skin, slowly but implacably, nerves unravel, cell walls buckle, messages go astray. Like gravity, like entropy, the rules of decay are printed in small type on our ticket of admission into the world.

The body is scarcely more durable than the reflection of a shadowy face in the night window. So where am I to turn during these unclocked hours before dawn? If there is no room for hope in the cramped house of the skin, and no security in the glimmerings of the mind, then what abides? Does anything persist, any knot more stubborn than bone, any force more steadfast than thought? The question drives me to set down my mug of tea, extinguish the kitchen light, and go outside into the dark.

·₊*

I might have walked into a cave, the dark is so deep. No light shines from the neighboring houses, nor from the moon, long since gone down, nor from the stars, blanked out by clouds. My eyes could be shut, for all the news they gather. Descending the steps into our backyard, I push against the darkness as against the weight of black water.

My eyes may be empty, but my ears quickly fill. The air sizzles with insect song. Crickets and grasshoppers warn and woo, rubbing their musical legs. They make the sound of beans rattling in a pan, tiny bells ringing on the ankles of dancers, fingers raked over the teeth of combs, waves rolling cobbles on the shore. Dozens of species combine to make this amorous hullabaloo. If I were to focus on the chirp of the snowy tree cricket, as one might pick out the oboe from an orchestra, and if I were to count the number of beats in fifteen seconds, then add that number to thirty-seven, the sum would roughly equal the temperature in Fahrenheit. I have tried this many times, and insect and thermometer usually agree within a few degrees. But on this muggy night I do not care to know the temperature, much as I admire the crickets for keeping track.

I hear no human sounds, amorous or otherwise, except the brief wail of a baby and the long wail of a siren. Cats bicker, without much enthusiasm. Now and again birds pipe up fretfully, as if reminding all within earshot that their trees are occupied. They will not be singing for some while yet. When baby, siren, cats, and birds fall silent, the insects own the air.

Listening, I cease to feel the weight of black water. I let myself walk out onto the lawn, trusting that the earth will uphold me, even though I cannot see the ground. The soil, baked hard by August, is lumpy under my bare feet. It smells of dust, dry and dull, as though it has never known the lushness of spring. The brittle grass licks my soles with a thousand feathery tongues. From the depths of my churchly childhood, the words of Isaiah (40:6–8) rise up:

All flesh is grass,
> and all its beauty is like the flower of the field.
The grass withers, the flower fades,
> when the breath of the Lord blows upon it;
> surely the people is grass.
The grass withers, the flower fades;
> but the word of our God will stand for ever.

Whoever composed that verse must have spent time down in the pit, wondering what does not fade, what will stand forever.

In lines that are familiar even to the unchurchly, Jesus converted Isaiah's warning into a promise: "Consider the lilies, how they grow; they neither toil nor spin; yet I tell you, even Solomon in all his glory was not arrayed like one of these. But if God so clothes the grass which is alive in the field today and tomorrow is thrown into the oven, how much more will he clothe you, O men of little faith!"

(Luke 12:27–28). Indeed, grass has been well clothed for more than a hundred million years. Persistent, nourishing grass! Brother to corn, sister to rice, cousin to wheat! In the darkness, the voices of Isaiah and Jesus speak to me like rival angels, one saying *Look how grass withers under the breath of August,* the other saying *Yes, but look how it pushes up numberless fresh blades each May.*

My frisky mind keeps darting off, loping through a lifetime of books, raiding memory, jumping ahead into the future, visiting countries where I have never set foot, zigzagging through the cosmos. And why not? When the fiddling of a cricket is tuned to the temperature, which is driven by the weather, which is linked to the earth's tilting spin, which is governed by all the matter in the universe, why shouldn't one's mind gambol about? Only risky, roving thought can be adequate to such a world.

While my mind rushes hither and yon, however, my body stays put. For the flesh there is no past or future, there is only this instant of contact, here, now. Heart pumps. Muscles twitch. Ears fill with indecipherable song. I lift my face and swallow some of the boggy air. With it comes the fruity smell of oak, released like a long held secret from the pile of split logs. I smell the rank sweetness of the compost bin, where apple cores and watermelon rinds deliquesce back toward dirt. I stroke the limestone blocks that hem in the wildflower bed. The flowers have faded but the stones endure, sandpapery to the touch. All the while, August heat clings to my limbs like damp wool.

As my eyes open their shutters to the dark, I dimly make out the twin trunks of our backyard maples. I shuffle to the nearer tree and read the braille of the bark with my fingers. Roots hump beneath my feet. Overhead, leaves form a canopy of black lace. I press my cheek and chest against the sharp ridges of the bark and wrap my arms around the trunk. My hands do not meet, the maple is so stout.

Once again, my mind sets off on its rambles. I remember hugging my Mississippi grandmother, her dresses made from flour sacking, her waist larger than the circle of my child's arms. I think of the goitrous, trembling, marvelous woman who taught me in high school biology class the parts of trees—heartwood and sapwood, phloem and cambium, stomata, rootlet, bud. I remember stroking the creamy flanks of sycamores on the banks of the Mahoning before that river was dammed. I think of the women in northern India who preserved their forest from loggers by hugging trees. Over our dead bodies, the women said, and meant it. Their struggle came to be known as Chipko, a Hindi expression meaning "embrace our trees."

If Ruth were to wake and come to the window and see me clasping a maple, would she be jealous? Would she fear losing me to the wood nymphs? Would she think I had become a druid? Or would she merely laugh at her ridiculous, moody husband? I do the laughing for her. My guffaw spreads ripples of silence through the crowd of insects. The spell broken, I unclasp the tree and stand back, hitching up my baggy shorts. I am comforted, although by whom or what I cannot say.

Comforted, I lie down on the lawn, and the blades prick the skin of my back and legs. I loaf and invite my soul. It is too dark for observing a spear of summer grass, yet I cannot help but remember Whitman's "Song of Myself":

A child said *What is the grass?* fetching it to me with full
hands;
How could I answer the child? I do not know what it is
any more than he.

Grass might be "the beautiful uncut hair of graves," Whitman speculates, yet he goes on to affirm that

The smallest sprout shows there is really no death,
And if ever there was it led forward life, and does
not wait at the end to arrest it,
And ceas'd the moment life appear'd.
All goes onward and outward, nothing collapses,
And to die is different from what any one supposed,
and luckier.

Instead of whistling in the dark, I sing. Lying there on my six feet of earth, I am reassured not so much by Whitman's words as by the shapely energy they appeal to—the chorusing crickets, the surging trees, the vigorous grass. My skin carries the bite marks of bark. My throat carries the aroma of cooking compost. My ears ring with the night gossip of birds. The darkness brims over with life. Thus I scratch my way up out of the pit into the arms of the world.

·*·

In the memorable phrasing of the Letter to the Hebrews (11:1), "faith is the assurance of things hoped for, the conviction of things not seen." By that measure, and by most others, I am a man of little faith. In the dark night of the soul, I reach out to assure myself of things not seen. I must lay my hands on the side of the tree, must feel the prick of grass on my skin, must smell the dirt, must sing to myself a brave lullaby in order to sustain my hopes.

What do I hope for? Eternal life, I suppose. By that I mean something besides immortality—although, like all creatures not maddened by pain, I am hooked on the habit of living. The eternal life I seek is not some after time, some other place, but awareness of eternity in this moment and this place. What I crave is contact with the force that moves and shapes all there is or has been or will be.

The earth and our bodies, by casting shadows, seem to be the opposite of light. But if you have gazed up through the leaves of a tree at the sky, if you have watched the jeweled crests of waves, or held a shimmering fish in your hand, or lifted your palm against the sun and seen ruby light blazing through the flesh of your squeezed fingers, you know that matter is filled with fire. Matter *is* fire, in slow motion. Einstein taught us as much, and bomb testers keep proving it with cataclysmic explosions. The resistant stuff we touch and walk on and eat, the resistant stuff we are, blood and bone, is not the opposite of light but light's incarnation.

The Taoist book of wisdom, *The Secret of the Golden Flower,* speaks about a condition of utter clarity and selflessness as "living midnight." I don't know a word of the original Chinese, and I might well misread the translation, but I am haunted by this phrase. Living midnight: to face oblivion, to drown in the annihilating water, to dwell without fear or fret at the still center. Hardest of all is to live *through* midnight, to accept the knowledge of one's own private extinction and still return to daylight charged with passion and purpose.

·.*

The man who dances in the backyard with an invisible lover, and then comes in the house humming to breakfast with his family, is the same one who was shaken like a rag by dread in the depths of the night.

"Hi, Pop," Eva says as I enter the kitchen.

"Morning, old guy," says Jesse.

"Did you have a bad night?" asks Ruth, who notices whenever I leave bed early.

"Not so bad," I answer, and then, considering, I add, "a good night, really."

I kiss their shining heads, each in turn. Their faces, so dear and mysterious, tilt up at me. Their skin glows from sleep. No, not only from sleep. They glow steadily, my wife and daughter and son, this morning as always, with a radiance that my wakefulness helps me to see.

·.*

This is no happy ending, merely an interlude, a reprieve. My vision will dim once more, and I will have to clear my sight. Dread will seize me by the throat. When the need comes on me, I will go outside.

The sudden fierce grip of fear was once thought to be the mischievous work of Pan, the god of wildness, and thus we still speak of feeling panic. I may be perverse, but I find myself soothed rather than frightened by wildness. I am reassured to feel one juice flowing through my fingers and the branches of the maple and the flickering grass. Pantheism has taken a beating since the rise of the great monotheistic religions. I believe there is only one power, one shaping urge, but I also believe that it infuses everything—the glistening track of the snail along with the gleaming eye of the fawn, the grain in the oak, the froth on the creek, the coiled proteins in my blood and in yours, the mind that strings together these words and the mind that reads them.

The only sure antidote to oblivion is the creation. So I loop my sentences around the trunks of maples, hook them into the parched soil, anchor them to rock, to moon and stars, wrap them tenderly around the ankles of those I love. From down in the pit I give a tug, to make sure my rope of words is firmly hooked into the world, and then up I climb.

HEART OF THE SKY

JENNIFER H. WESTERMAN

I became a mother in the season of long nights. The equinox had balanced out light and dark, and then evening came earlier and night settled, deeper and cooler, in the Blue Ridge Mountains. I had been sleepless for weeks, little kicks and punches emanating from my belly, tiny feet and knees and elbows asserting themselves in accidental gestures. In my grandmother's words for the aimless walking of restless nights, I "prowled the floor." Some nights were so obscured by fog that our house seemed to be floating on a cloudbank; other nights were still and clear.

During my night waking, I memorized the arrangement of hillside lights from distant houses, observed star patterns, witnessed the harvest moon and then the hunter's moon. I heard a bobcat shriek and cough in the meadow and hound dogs howl from their night kennels. Ivory yellow lights from the nearest valley town illuminated contours of surrounding mountainsides. The darkest time before sunrise seemed mine alone to feel the weight of life inside me, to visualize the arc of a little eyebrow or the curve of closed fingers in a tiny fist.

Our daughter, Iris, was born during an early snowstorm three nights past November's full moon. We drove home from the hospital as if in slow motion, acutely attuned to the road, her breathing, our own heart rhythms. Our world was suddenly alight in a beautiful way like icy snow in moonlight. This vulnerable creature had just arrived on land from the sea inside me, and waves of worry and promise crashed in my head. As I recovered from an unplanned cesarean delivery, even the idea of walking was painful. Iris and I nestled together on our downstairs sofa in front of the fireplace, while my husband slept on a pallet on the floor beside us, ready to rock our daughter in his arms when I could not.

When I had gathered more strength and could hold her and wander through the house when she awoke at night, I did. I tried to find the rhythm in my movements that would both soothe her and keep myself alert. Did she recognize the way the floors creaked and popped or remember the sway of my hips? Did she feel my breath on her head and know it as mine? I whispered to her the names of things cast in silhouette by the moon's glow: rhododendrons, bare dogwood, bird feeder, grape arbor. Looking skyward, I sought the fantastic nebula nursery in Orion, where thousands of stars are born. In hushed tones, I told her stories about past nights when I had other company.

·.*

In the hazy blue glow of a winter night, I rocked Iris in my arms and told her the story of the darkest night I had ever witnessed. I once lived in a remote village in the altiplano region of Guatemala where I taught environmental education classes for children. Steep mountains, pine trees, and red soil reminded me of my Appalachian home. In this community of about twenty adobe houses, a couple of *tiendas,* and a rustic schoolhouse, I rented a room from a kind family.

The room—left vacant when their son slipped into the United States under the cover of a moonless night—was its own structure apart from the main house, up a hill by the sheep pens.

I loved the company of my host mother, Doña Tia, and her young girls. They would come up early in the mornings and sit in the dooryard with me. "Why don't you have children?" the girls asked me. Having grown weary of hearing this question for the past two years that I had lived in Central America, I told them that all the men I knew were too ugly to have children with. We all laughed, and then the girls translated their mother's Mayan words into Spanish for me. Doña Tia said, "Someday the heart of the sky will bring you children."

There was no electricity in the village or for many miles in either direction. I did not see the skyglow of distant towns, no misty lights thrown out from windows. At night, the highlands were cold, sometimes freezing. I climbed into my rope bed and pulled the hood of my sleeping bag tightly around my head and sometimes slept with mittens and a hat. Often I awoke to thin sheets of frozen water in the *pila,* a communal basin where we washed dishes and clothes and faces. Once a week, after nightfall, Doña Tia would go inside the family *tuj* with a modest bundle of firewood. The tuj was a small, igloo-shaped bathhouse. After the family had bathed, Doña Tia would come to my room and signal that it was my turn.

The first time that I ever bathed in the tuj the night sky was the color of dark indigo and deep eggplant purple. I imagine the depths of the ocean are these shades. It was beyond dark, save the stars. Thousands upon thousands of stars densely packed the sky with scintillating light. The expanse of the sky was profoundly clear, like the moment when I looked into my husband's eyes as our daughter was born. It was as if the whole of the universe spread over me like a canopy and all the world beneath it teemed with life and story.

I gathered my *guacal,* a gourd used for dipping water, a towel, and soap and crawled through the short tunnel opening of the tuj. Inside the adobe walls, the room opened up, and there were wide, wood planks, raised up slightly off the earthen floor on stones. A large black kettle was suspended over a fire, and the smell of damp earth and wood smoke permeated the warm air. I added hot water from the kettle to the cooler water in the basin and used my guacal to ladle up the heated, sooty water. It had been a week since I had bathed, a week since I felt hot water on my skin. I poured the water over me and felt newly born. I thought that I was utterly alone in the world beneath a sky as wide as the sea. A tremendous feeling of loneliness overwhelmed me. Then I heard a familiar, gentle cough from just outside the tuj. It was Doña Tia's cough, and she was watching over me as my own mother would when I needed reassurance that she and I watched the same moon even though we lived a great distance apart. When I crawled out of the tuj, Doña Tia gave me a blanket, while she pulled her own heavy shawl tightly around her shoulders. It was a moment of absolute peace. We could see our breath floating out into the night. We stood in silence beneath clusters of light-birthing stars overhead.

Would my daughter know a dark sky such as this? Were some of those same stars above my daughter and me now? With Iris in my arms, I sensed the turn of a telescope lens bringing the world into close range. I imagined that she would someday see the detail, would know the natural world as it unfolds beneath the night sky, and during another wakeful night I told her a story of sea turtles.

· ₊ *

I had worked as a park ranger at an isolated state park on the southern coast of Virginia. The park's nine-mile shoreline comprised one of the few remaining stretches of undeveloped coast on the eastern seaboard. A wildlife refuge to the north, the ocean to the east, a bay to the west, and protected lands to the south bordered the park. There were a few primitive campsites, no potable water. No cars were permitted to enter the park. I lived in a plain cabin on the bay side. A whip-poor-will would nestle in the middle of the path to my cabin and announce the night to the scrub oak forest. The air smelled salty and fertile.

I watched meteor showers from the dark beach and swam in the moonlit ocean. With a stroke of my arm or the turn of a wave, bioluminescent creatures would shimmer through the sea. On a summer night, a loggerhead sea turtle returned to this beach. Her flippers swept the sand away in great arcs as she crawled to the dune line. There, she dug a "flask," a deep nest in the sand, and laid a clutch of more than one hundred round, white eggs. Under the dome of the night sky, she covered the nest with sand and crawled slowly back into the ocean.

A high mortality rate for endangered sea turtles made human intervention necessary, so as soon as I spotted her crawl, I notified a local team from the maritime museum and the marine sciences institute. The team came to gather the eggs from the nest. Carefully, the scientists placed the eggs in a special cooler, paying heed to the order in which the eggs had been deposited. For nearly two months, the eggs safely incubated. And then, as tiny, phototactic hatchlings, they were returned to the shore to be released into their native habitat.

It was a cool night when we sent the hatchlings home. They were ancient sea turtles in exact miniature. Smaller than the palm of my hand, bigger than the palm of my daughter's hand. We carefully lifted the hatchlings from their coolers and placed them on the sand. With what seemed like an impossible instinct, these wee little beings headed straight for the ocean, now part of the 150-million-year story of sea turtles. Undaunted by the crash of waves or the tide's pull, the hatchlings followed the moonlight and starlight reflected off the ocean and dove in unhesitatingly. Their infant flippers would swim nonstop until they reached the Sargasso Sea, where they would drift and grow for many years suspended in their own amniotic sea. We stood on the dark beach and sent up our hopes for their survival to the stars.

The winter solstice was approaching. During my daughter's first month, I had spoken very softly other stories of the night: the ephemeral night-blooming cereus of the Sonoran Desert; the full moon rolling across the knife's edge of Mount Katahdin; the glowing of earthshine in Logan Canyon as the crescent moon wrapped the full moon in its arms like a baby; the flickering of northern lights above Canadian lakes. I did not tell Iris quietly of my fear that she would not experience these mysteries. That her night skies may be too obscured by artificial lights for her to stand beneath the dark dome of the world and see a multitude of stars, a projection of story in their constellations. We already live in a world where these unnatural lights pitch shadows across our galaxy and disorient tiny, ocean-bound sea turtles. When she is prowling the floor with her own daughter, will she step outside into the cool night and look up? What stories will she whisper to the night?

CODA:
WHAT THE SOLUTION
WOULD LOOK LIKE

CHRISTIAN LUGINBUHL

"When the great earth, abandoning day, rolls up the deeps of the heavens and the universe, a new door opens for the human spirit, and there are few so clownish that some awareness of the mystery of being does not touch them as they gaze" (Henry Beston).

∙.*

I don't think there's anybody who isn't inspired by a starry night. They may not necessarily think of themselves as stargazers—they don't go out and set up a telescope with the purpose of spending hours looking at the sky—but they're still moved by the starscape of the night sky, and it gives them a perspective even if they think of it only for five minutes.

Yet one common mistake made about the problem of light pollution, of losing night, is that it is pigeonholed as an astronomer's or stargazer's concern. This misconception narrows the problem into a worry for an elite or peculiar few. Nobody ever seems to make the mistake of thinking that we protect Yellowstone or the Grand Canyon just for geologists and rockhounds.

Another misconception is that the problem is insoluble because it's attached to the inevitability of development, not just in this country but worldwide. As we add more people and as standards of living are raised and more economic activity happens and more of it happens at night—gosh, is there any way around it?

It's not as intractable as that makes it sound. An awful lot of the light that ends up in the sky—probably more than three-fourths of it—is not inevitable. If we can get light to be more effectively used for the purposes that it's intended—give people enough light to see by and to accomplish whatever task or security that they want, but not five times as much or ten times as much—we could make huge progress. I'm not making numbers up; the magnitude of the misuse of light is so large that if you address it you can really make substantial improvements in the sky, even without changing the fundamental way society and people relate to night.

Compared to the things that we grapple with as a society, like war and poverty, or even something more germane like air pollution, difficult as those are, you see in contrast how simple solving light pollution is. If only we would start using light sensibly and then begin replacing old lights at the same time—all the lights that were put up insensibly—we could bring it to a standstill, even reverse it.

∵

It's safe to say that virtually everywhere the problem continues to get worse. One way to measure the extent of light pollution is to ask, can people see the Milky Way? That is a threshold where the sky is in the transition of turning from something stunning and inspirational to something mundane, something close, almost like that tapestry over your head that the ancients imagined the celestial sphere to be, with stars painted on it. In Europe and the United States, between half and two-thirds of the people live where they cannot see the Milky Way. That's a large fraction. Certainly most people living in cities of over 100,000 cannot see the Milky Way. And the fraction's increasing; our population is still moving to large cities, and our cities continue to grow. More and more people are losing the night, not only because they're moving to the cities but also because the amount of light used *per person* is growing. We're deciding it's more important to light up more things, and more brightly.

An obvious example is what has happened to service stations in recent years. A lot of people would certainly notice that they've increased their lighting levels by startling amounts, and actually the ratio is five or ten times as much as they used to use, twenty years ago. Parking lots too are getting more and more brightly illuminated.

Whereas it used to be considered acceptable to have a parking lot lit to twenty times full moonlight, now it's common to go ten times that, two hundred times full moonlight.

Why is this is happening? To me that's the question of our relation to the night. As Henry Beston wrote, "Our fantastic civilization has fallen out of touch with many aspects of nature, and with none more completely than with night." He said that in 1928, which is just stunning. In 1928 there were hardly any lights out there—the rural electrification of this country didn't happen until the 1940s and 1950s. So he was talking about it before then, when modern electric lighting was just beginning to invade our cities. We didn't have shopping malls and roadways everywhere that were always lit up, not to anything like the extent we have now.

·.*

We're becoming increasingly isolated from the night, and as we become isolated from the night it becomes strange and fearsome to us. There's always been an undercurrent of human fear of the dark. But people who are afraid of the dark now aren't thinking about bears and tigers, generally, because they're living in cities or areas where such large predators have been completely eliminated. Even in the remote areas of the United States, most predators have been eliminated—wolves, for example. What we substitute is the fear of crime and the fear of each other.

That's underlying a lot of this increasing lighting. And it's all reflective of growing out of touch with the night. We don't have a realistic evaluation of what is dangerous. Crime at night is not actually much greater than it used to be, and in some places it's less than it used to be, but we feel that it's worse. When you ask lighting designers why they use so much light, if it's really necessary, they oftentimes say, "This is what our customers ask for, it makes them feel secure." They say, "Our business is to respond to our customers' needs, and if they say they need light, then we give them light."

We need to educate people to reach more realistic conclusions about their risks at night and how lighting can help to split apart the difference between feeling secure and actually being safe. You can double or triple or increase by ten times the light and people might feel safer, but they are probably not safer. They may actually be less safe than if there was no fixed lighting at all. And there's a cost associated with the approach, a cost measured not just in money for paying the electric bills. There are resources consumed, air pollution produced, light pollution, the loss of the night skies and their inspiration, increasing isolation of all of us from the natural world at night. And it feeds on itself—people aren't going to ask to preserve the stars if they've never seen them. The fewer people who see them, the fewer people who will ask the question about whether all this lighting is necessary. Joseph Wood Krutch—and he was speaking about sound and silence but he could just as well have been speaking about lighting—wrote that if human beings no longer have access to quiet, inevitably it must happen that people will no longer miss the quiet, because they adapt to the conditions that they live in.

Once you identify a real safety issue that you can address with lighting, it can be done with lighting that has much less impact on the night sky. We usually just throw up light that is glaring, wasteful, oftentimes too much—lighting that may actually compromise safety. Take glare—if light shines into your eyes, it makes things less visible. It always does. By definition, glare is blinding light. So we put up light to help see something on the ground, or behind the bush, or the other side of the street, but it also shines into your eyes, which takes away from visibility. With glary lighting we actually create darkness, where we may have seen fine without the added light.

·٭·

On a community-wide average with all the different kinds of lighting we use, from roadways to billboards to service stations to signs—everything mixed together—about 10 percent of the light emitted by fixtures goes directly into the sky. This wasted light never lights anybody's way, never provides any safety or security at all—it just goes straight up. Ten percent. Now, that doesn't sound like much at first, but think about it a little more. That tells you that 90 percent goes downward and actually hits the ground. On average the ground reflects about 15 percent. So 90 percent goes down, 15 percent reflects back up, which gives you 13.5 percent reflecting off the ground back into the sky, added to the 10 percent already headed straight up from the fixtures. So roughly half of the light getting into the sky never touched the ground—it's completely wasted. All of a sudden you realize that nearly half of the light that's causing skyglow doesn't need to be there at all—half of it! That's a much more impressive figure. So imagine taking a community that has an average 10 percent unshielded light going straight up, and replacing all the lighting with fixtures that put all the light downward. Immediately your skyglow would drop to half. That's just stunning.

And further, if you now talk about questions such as parking lots that are twenty times as bright as they need to be for safety purposes—and parking lots are probably between 50 and 75 percent of the lighting we use outdoors—if you bring those lighting levels down from twenty times what's necessary to just what is necessary, that's an even larger decrease, that's a ten or more times decrease.

If we really looked at lighting sensibly, if we really did get better shielding, if we really did get lighting levels that are adequate but not excessive, we could make huge strides in returning the stars to our rural and even our urban areas.

.⋆˙

How do we respond to objections that this would cost too much? One is the less aggressive way, which is simply to wait. It's going to happen anyway—lighting fixtures don't last that long. When you first get into the business and you feel impatient, as we all do, you tend to think gosh, that fixture just went up, it's brand-spanking new, it's shiny, it's made of heavy-duty metal and glass, it's good quality—it seems like it's going to last forever. But twenty-five years from now that thing's going to look horrible. It's going to be worn out, it's going to be hard to find parts for it, it's going to be time to replace it. So what we need to do is to get legal standards in place that will require that when these lights are changed naturally they are replaced with fixtures that are well shielded.

The other response is that you don't wait but instead say okay, it's not that old but it's so bad we're going fix it. Technology has improved enough in terms of the efficiency of the lamps and fixtures that in most cases the energy savings that you can get by increasing the efficiency of the lighting—and still providing just as good or better visibility—will pay back the capital expenditure of the replacement within five or ten years, typically, through the savings of the energy.

For example, a fixture that shines 10 percent light upward usually is spraying light near the horizontal and causing a lot of glare. You can remove all of that. You cut the energy use of that fixture down to a half or three-quarters of what it was. That's a substantial energy savings, and one that's only going to increase as energy costs continue to rise. And that energy savings is going to accrue endlessly as you use the light. Every time you use the light you save money. That's one of the things that people tend to forget when they do lighting—they look at the cost of the fixtures and they may look at the cost of the lamp, and if they are really farsighted they sometimes think about paying somebody to change those bulbs. But what they forget is that most of the cost of providing lighting is the electrical cost, because that adds up nightly. Over the lifetime of the fixtures, say twenty years, about 90 percent of the cost that you've spent to have that lighting has been the electricity. Therefore, small savings in that area can really pay back the costs of the installation.

·.*

The battle for night skies will come down to this: to how many people is it going to become important enough to preserve a view of the night sky? Because only if people demand it will it happen. I don't think getting a few thousand people to join a dark sky association, or a few thousand members of a professional lighting organization persuaded that dark skies are wonderful is going to do it. That will be part of what needs to happen, but the lighting profession in particular is driven from the bottom up. They are not educators, they are not philosophers, they are not visionaries. They respond to what their clients want, and if their clients don't want stars, then they'll deliver products that don't give them stars. The battle for dark skies will be won only through the hearts of the people, not by technical solutions imposed by lighting professionals or governments. However persuasive the International Dark-Sky Association might become, however many professionals we might convince that good lighting and dark skies are the greatest, we won't make any progress at all unless everyday people not only care about it but care enough about it to demand it.

You may not need to convince 75 percent of the people that the stars are important; it may be some smaller threshold. That helps to inspire me because that has happened here in Flagstaff. Only a small fraction of the people are actively and persistently involved in raising awareness, and we tend to focus on the aesthetic side of it, not the technical. We try to get people out to look at the night sky, to raise their eyes above the horizontal, to look through telescopes, to be aware of it. The result has been surprising. In local editorials and articles, for example, that don't really seem to be about stars or lighting, the quality of our starry night skies has just become part of the conversation. General awareness has shifted from near blindness to the night and stars to a place where dark star-filled skies are important for everyone and worthy of protection. Stars are a part of what our community is about. As we sometimes say to schoolchildren, "The stars are in your backyard."

It really is a tractable problem, in fact more than tractable. We ought to be able to improve it at the same time that we grow, and improve it from every perspective, not just better skies, but lower energy use, better visibility, and here's another one: a better nighttime aesthetic of our communities. We've come to accept glaring lighting as the standard and we don't even notice it. We can improve the appearance of our communities. Good lighting looks nice.

Increasingly, communities are concerned with their aesthetic character. They spend lots of time trying to preserve the local flavor of the architecture, writing codes to keep signs from obliterating the visibility of the buildings or the landscape, talking about burying power lines because of the ugliness of the poles and wires strung all over our daytime landscape. But nobody seems to think much about night. What determines what our communities look like when the sun goes down? How we use lighting.

Many communities don't want lighting like Las Vegas, blinking and flashing, dominating the night. They think that's distracting or aesthetically not pleasing. But they haven't thought, Is our street lighting glaring? How about the lighting on the commercial properties near roads? Is it interfering with the ability to see—is it shining in people's eyes and making it hard to see pedestrians? Is it ugly? Architects spend a lot of time thinking about lighting indoors. They care about the hues and the colors and intensities, and if there is enough lighting for you to do what you want. When was the last time you saw a living room or bedside lamp without a shade, glaring straight into your eyes? But we haven't made the transition to the outdoor environment with that kind of sensibility.

·.·

The diminishment of the human imagination, the diminishment of our understanding of our place in the universe—these costs are very hard to calculate. What happens when a Henry Beston is born today but never gets an exposure—whatever it is that happened in his life that made him sensitive and able to see so clearly—what happens when that person is born today but doesn't get that exposure, because of light pollution? What do we lose as a society, as a people? It's not something you can put numbers on. And our monetary, cost-driven culture would say if you can't put a number on it, don't talk to me. It's too abstract to grapple with—or worse, it has no value. But abstract and difficult things are some of the most important things—in fact, from my perspective the most important things. Certainly, like any human being I need to provide for my family, and that entails an involvement with the cash economy of our culture, but there is a poet in me that yearns to be fed, and I'm fed by a gaze at the night sky.

Many people say that walking in a forest is nourishing to them, and they're not talking about eating, and they're not talking about botanical knowledge—it's a deeper connection than that. Many also say that the existence of wilderness even where they do not visit and don't expect to visit nourishes them. And while it doesn't seem as you walk down the street that there is a preponderance of people to whom this is important, maybe it has crossed that tipping point, to where it's just been accepted that protecting forests and wilderness is part of what we're about.

If we could get night to that place. Dark, natural night, filled with an infinity of stars.

We have not yet begun to slow the growth of light pollution in this country. We need to slow it down, stop it, and turn it around, and that can happen if we can get to that tipping point.

We know what the solution would look like. It doesn't require hundreds of millions of dollars of research or digging up billions of tons of contaminated soil and transporting it for cleansing. Replace or remove a poor light fixture and the light pollution it made disappears—at the speed of light. It's really very simple.

CONTRIBUTORS

THOMAS BECKNELL grew up on the barren high plains of eastern Wyoming and the hills of western Nebraska. He received his PHD from the University of Iowa and teaches courses in American literary history and environmental writing at Bethel University. The Boundary Waters Canoe Area Wilderness of northern Minnesota has become his favorite retreat for contemplating the night sky.

MICHAEL P. BRANCH is a professor of literature and environment at the University of Nevada, Reno. He is a cofounder and past president of the Association for the Study of Literature and Environment (ASLE), book review editor of the journal *ISLE: Interdisciplinary Studies in Literature and Environment,* and coeditor of the University of Virginia Press book series Under the Sign of Nature: Explorations in Ecocriticism. He has published more than one hundred articles and reviews on nature writing and environmental literature, and his most recent book is *Reading the Roots: American Nature Writing Before Walden.* Mike lives with his wife and two daughters at six thousand feet in the desert north of Reno, where the Great Basin and the Sierra Nevada meet under a big, dark sky.

JAMES BREMNER has worked as a mathematician and software engineer in Europe, Africa, and North America for the mining, medical, and telecom industries. He now lives in Ontario, and writes, "As a young man my sports were of the kind now called 'extreme,' principally rock climbing and motor biking. Although I am now involved in the more sedate activities of sailboat racing and cross-country skiing, there still seems little point to me in a sport without a tinge of fear."

CHRISTOPHER COKINOS is an assistant professor of English and adjunct assistant professor of environment and society at Utah State University, where he also edits *Isotope: A Journal of Literary Nature and Science Writing.* He is the author of *Hope Is the Thing With Feathers: A Personal Chronicle of Vanished Birds.* He often stargazes from his "backyard along the Blacksmith

Fork River in semi-rural southern Cache Valley. The Bear River Range rises to our east, and so over the mountains and above the canyon the sky is pretty dark. The Milky Way is still visible from where I live, and I hope we'll keep it way." His essay, "A Backyard History of Light," first appeared in *Turnrow* (Winter 2007).

JOHN DANIEL is the author of eight books of poetry, essays, and memoir, most recently *Rogue River Journal: A Winter Alone.* From his home in the inland foothills of the Oregon Coast Range, the radiance of greater Eugene dilutes the eastern sky at night, but to the west, a starry darkness shows between towering silhouettes of Douglas firs—when it isn't raining or trying to rain. Daniel and his wife also spend time at a cottage in the sagebrush steppe of eastern Oregon, where, he says, "on the right nights, the open sky is a smoky, studded texture of starlight you can almost reach up and touch." His essay, "In Praise of Darkness," first appeared in *Southwest Review* (Fall 2007).

JAN DEBLIEU's latest book is *Year of the Comets: A Journey From Sadness to the Stars.* She is also the author of *Wind: How the Flow of Air Has Shaped Life, Myth, and the Land,* for which she won the 1999 John Burroughs Medal for outstanding nature writing. She lives on North Carolina's Outer Banks.

ALISON HAWTHORNE DEMING's most recent books are *Writing the Sacred Into the Real* and *Genius Loci.* She teaches creative writing at the University of Arizona and lives near Agua Caliente Hill in Tucson just outside the lightshed of the city. She spends summers on Grand Manon Island in the Bay of Fundy, where the skies are so dark at night that the Milky Way is a superhighway of luminosity.

WILLIAM L. FOX has published numerous books on cognition and landscape, and has received fellowships from the Guggenheim Foundation, the National Endowment for the Humanities, and the National Science Foundation. He is a fellow of the Royal Geographical Society and has also published fifteen collections of poetry, as well as written several monographs on art and photography. Stymied by an inability to even balance a checkbook, much less perform tensor calculus, he gave up his early ambitions to be an astrophysicist and settled for writing.

DAVID GESSNER is the author of six books, including *Return of the Osprey* and *Sick of Nature*. He taught environmental writing at Harvard, edits the literary journal *Ecotone*, and teaches creative writing at the University of North Carolina, Wilmington. He has moved from Cape Cod to Wrightsville Beach, North Carolina, where spotlights shine out like suns and you can see your shadow at midnight.

RAY GONZALEZ has won numerous awards for his nine books of poetry, which include *The Hawk Temple at Tierra Grande* and *Consideration of the Guitar: New and Selected Poems*. His poetry has appeared in the 1999, 2000, and 2003 editions of *The Best American Poetry*. He is the author of two collections of essays, *The Underground Heart: A Return to a Hidden Landscape*, and *Memory Fever*, a memoir about growing up in the Southwest. He has written two collections of short stories, *The Ghost of John Wayne* and *Circling the Tortilla Dragon*, and is the editor of twelve anthologies. He has served as poetry editor of the *Bloomsbury Review* for twenty-two years and founded LUNA, a poetry journal, in 1998. He is a professor in the MFA Creative Writing Program at the University of Minnesota in Minneapolis.

SHAUN T. GRIFFIN is the author of several collections of poetry, including *Bathing in the River of Ashes*. He lives in Virginia City, Nevada.

SUSAN HANSON is a native Texan who grew up on the central Gulf Coast and has lived in the Hill Country for more than thirty years. A resident of San Marcos, on the southeastern edge of the Edwards Plateau, she teaches English at Texas State University and serves as co-chaplain for the Lutheran-Episcopal Campus Ministry there. Her essay collection, *Icons of Loss and Grace: Moments From the Natural World*, was published in 2004. *What Wildness Is This: Women Write About the Southwest*, a collection she coedited, was released in 2007. Susan lives with her husband, Larry, and has a grown daughter in Austin. Because her home is surrounded by live oaks, Hanson typically watches the night sky from the clearing at the end of her driveway. She worries about the encroachment of the city on her rural neighborhood, especially the lights from the nearby outlet malls, but so far the sky directly overhead and to the west remains dark.

GARY HARRISON is a professor of English at the University of New Mexico, where he teaches courses in literature and the environment, British and Irish romanticism, literary theory, and world literature. He is the coeditor of two major anthologies of world literature, the author of a book on William Wordsworth's poetry, and the author of several articles on early-nineteenth-century literature and culture. After moving around the country for many years, Gary has lived in Albuquerque, New Mexico, since 1987. He adds as an epilogue to his essay, "Night Light," that the management of the nearby store "finally agreed to, and completed, installing fully shielded lights in the parking lot behind our house; they even put up a noise-barrier to mitigate the noise from and to conceal behind a wall the refrigerator motors on the roof of their store. Lobbying can pay off."

From 1979 until 1999 **PHILIP HISCOCK** was the archivist at the Memorial University of Newfoundland Folklore and Language Archive; since then he has been on the faculty of MUN's Department of Folklore in St. John's, at the most easterly point of Canada. His degrees are in dialectology and folklore, and his current research areas include popular song, local language, and regional legends. He often appears on radio and television discussing contemporary and traditional folklore. According to Hiscock, it does not take a long drive from St. John's to find good darkness. He and his wife spend part of their time in Ganny Cove Arm in Newfoundland's Trinity Bay. The Trinity Bay sky is wide, dark, full of stars, and sometimes noisy during showers of meteors.

ROBIN WALL KIMMERER is a professor on the faculty of Environmental and Forest Biology at the State University of New York College of Environmental Science and Forestry Department. *Gathering Moss: A Natural and Cultural History of Mosses,* her first book, won the 2005 John Burroughs Medal for outstanding nature writing.

LAURIE KUTCHINS has published widely in journals and anthologies, including the *Georgia Review,* the *New Yorker,* the *Southern Review,* the *Kenyon Review, Orion,* and *Ploughshares.* Her books of poetry include *Between Towns, The Night Path,* and *Slope of the Child Everlasting.* Regarding her essay for this collection, she writes, "I am grateful to Erich Neumann's interpretation of the Eros and Psyche story in *Amor and Psyche: The Psychic Development of the Feminine.*" She teaches at James Madison University in the Shenandoah Valley of Virginia and summers on the Wyoming-Idaho border. She grew up in central Wyoming, where, she reports, "night is even larger than the horizon."

KEN LAMBERTON's first book, *Wilderness and Razor Wire,* won the 2002 John Burroughs Medal for outstanding nature writing. He has published more than a hundred nature articles and essays, and was anthologized in *The Best American Science and Nature Writing 2000.* He since has published *Chiricahua Mountains: Bridging the Borders of Wildness* and *Beyond Desert Walls: Essays From Prison.* Lamberton lives with his wife and daughters "on the desert outskirts of Tucson, away from the city lights where I can see the stars most nights—I have a habit of always looking up when I'm out at night, probably simply to get my bearings. My favorite dark place to really see the night is in the Pinacate Desert of northern Sonora, Mexico, about three hours from Tucson."

GRETCHEN LEGLER is a professor in the Department of Humanities at the University of Maine at Farmington, where she teaches in the BFA program in creative writing. Work from her first collection of essays, *All the Powerful Invisible Things: A Sportswoman's Notebook,* has won two Pushcart Prizes and has been widely excerpted and anthologized. Her second book, *On the Ice: An Intimate Portrait of Life at McMurdo Station, Antarctica,* was published in 2005.

CHRISTIAN LUGINBUHL has been an astronomer at the U.S. Naval Observatory Flagstaff Station since 1981. He studied astronomy, physics, chemistry, and botany at Northern Arizona University, with graduate work in astronomy at Case Western Reserve University. He is a member of the American Astronomical Society, the Illuminating Engineering Society of North America, and serves on the board of directors for the International Dark-Sky Association (IDA). He has been principal author of many innovative outdoor lighting codes, as well as principal author and editor of the *IDA Outdoor Lighting Code Handbook.* His principal research in recent years concerns outdoor lighting, the ways it is used, how the details of its use contribute to skyglow, and how skyglow can be minimized. He sees the principal value of a dark night sky in the inspiration and perspective it offers, and not in its potential to further astronomical research.

ANNE MATTHEWS teaches environmental writing at Princeton University. She has written three books on distinctive American places undergoing rapid change: *Where the Buffalo Roam* describes the ongoing debate over turning portions of the Great Plains into a Buffalo Common; *Bright College Years* explores the American campus as a highly diverse environment; and *Wild Nights: Nature Returns to the City* considers the new and urgent meanings of urban ecology. She is originally from Madison, Wisconsin, and much prefers the starry night skies of the Midwestern uplands to those in the New York megalopolis.

KATHLEEN DEAN MOORE is best known for her books about our cultural and spiritual connections to wet, wild places—*Riverwalking, Holdfast,* and *The Pine Island Paradox.* Moore is Distinguished Professor of Philosophy at Oregon State University, where she teaches environmental ethics and directs the Spring Creek Project for Ideas, Nature, and the Written Word. Her home is on the wet side of the Cascade Mountains in Corvallis, Oregon, but she roams the rivers and inlets of the northwest Pacific coast with her family and sometimes with her students. Floating in small boats in the dark, she comes closest to the meaning of the night.

ROBERT MICHAEL PYLE writes essay, fiction, and poetry along a rainy tributary of the Lower Columbia River in southwest Washington. His fourteen books include *Wintergreen, The Thunder Tree, Where Bigfoot Walks, Chasing Monarchs, Walking the High Ridge,* and *Sky Time in Gray's River: Living for Keeps in a Forgotten Place,* as well as "a bunch of butterfly books." His essay-column "The Tangled Bank" appears in each issue of *Orion* magazine. One of the things he most appreciates about his rural dwelling place is its still-dark skies. In a county without a single traffic light and few streetlights, he can see stars, planets, and moon whenever the time of day and the clouds allow. Pyle has always enjoyed long night walks, both in cities and in the countryside. While his piece in this collection is a work of fiction, he says that "it gives some clear clues as to how the author came to know and love the night."

Writer, naturalist, and activist **JANISSE RAY** is the author of three books of literary nonfiction: *Ecology of a Cracker Childhood,* a memoir about growing up on a junkyard in the ruined longleaf pine ecosystem of the Southeast; *Wild Card Quilt: Taking a Chance on Home,* about community (human and wild); and, most recently, *Pinhook: Finding Wholeness in a Fragmented Land,* the story of a 750,000-acre wildland corridor between south Georgia and north Florida. She loves to experience night on full-moon paddles down the Altamaha River.

CHET RAYMO is professor emeritus at Stonehill College in Easton, Massachusetts. He is the author of a dozen books on science and nature, including *The Soul of the Night, An Intimate Look at the Night Sky* (from which "Why the Night Sky Is Dark" comes), and *Walking Zero: Discovering Cosmic Space and Time Along the Prime Meridian.* His weekly column "Science Musings" appeared in the *Boston Globe* from 1983 to 2003. His work has been widely anthologized, including in *The Norton Book of Nature Writing.* He is a winner of a 1998 Lannan Literary Award for his nonfiction work. He resides on the Web at www. sciencemusings.com.

CHRISTINA ROBERTSON has taught environmental literature, creative writing, and ecocomposition at the University of Nevada, Reno, and Colorado State University. She completed her MFA in fiction at CSU and her PHD in literature and the environment at UNR. She's currently at work on an environmental memoir. Chris lives in Reno with her husband, John. They watched the November 2002 Leonid meteor showers out in the Sierra Valley, over the ridge from Reno's casino haze. They often stargaze camped in Buckeye Canyon on the eastern slope of the Sierras. The best place to see the Milky Way might be where Chris grew up, in the West Kootenay region of southeastern British Columbia. "There," she claims, "the stars are still as thick as the mosquitoes."

SCOTT RUSSELL SANDERS has written numerous books, including *The Force of Spirit, Secrets of the Universe,* and most recently *A Private History of Awe.* He lives in Bloomington, Indiana, where he is professor of English at the University of Indiana. Sanders's contribution to this book comes from his essay "Earth's Body," which appears in his book *Staying Put: Making a Home in a Restless World.*

JOHN TALLMADGE is the author of numerous essays on nature, culture, literature, and human values, as well as three books, including *Meeting the Tree of Life: A Teacher's Path* and *The Cincinnati Arch: Learning From Nature in the City.* An editor and teacher with thirty years' experience in doctoral and undergraduate education, John lives in Cincinnati, Ohio, where he works in educational and literary consulting, for which he can be reached at www.johntallmadge.com.

MARK TREDINNICK is an Australian poet, essayist, and writing teacher. His books include *The Land's Wild Music* and *The Little Red Writing Book* (published in the United States in 2008 as *The Art of Prose*). Mark is also the editor of *A Place on Earth: An Anthology of Nature Writing From Australia and North America,* and his work has appeared in journals in Australia, the United States, and the United Kingdom. For many years, Mark lived in the Blue Mountains, west of Sydney. After a stint in the city, he now lives with his family in the southern highlands.

JENNIFER H. WESTERMAN is a doctoral student in the Literature and Environment Program at the University of Nevada, Reno. Prior to beginning her PHD program, she served as a Peace Corps volunteer in El Salvador (1997–99) and worked for state parks, the National Park Service, and the U.S. Forest Service from Maine to Arizona and many places in between. She currently teaches at Appalachian State University while working on her dissertation research in late-nineteenth- and early-twentieth-century American environmental and social justice literature. Jennifer and her husband, Jim, watch the night sky with their daughter, Iris, and son, Ansel, from Boone, North Carolina.

RESOUCES

All royalties from sales of this book will be used to support groups actively and effectively working on behalf of the night. Please consider learning more about their missions and donating to their work. These groups include:

INTERNATIONAL DARK-SKY ASSOCIATION (IDA)

The mission of the International Dark-Sky Association (IDA) is to preserve and protect the nighttime environment and our heritage of dark skies through quality outdoor lighting. IDA lists as its goal to "stop the adverse effects of light pollution on dark skies, including energy waste and the air and water pollution caused by energy waste; harm to human health; harm to nocturnal wildlife and ecosystems; reduced safety and security; reduced visibility at night; poor nighttime ambience; raise awareness about light pollution, its adverse effects, and its solutions; educate everyone, everywhere, about the values of quality outdoor lighting; help stop other threats to our view of the universe, such as radio frequency interference (RFI) and space debris." IDA works with "communities, astronomers, ecologists, and lighting professionals; we are active on local, national, and international stages . . . in conserving, preserving, and restoring our natural dark skies."

International Dark-Sky Association
3225 N. First Avenue, Tucson, Arizona 85719-2103, USA
Telephone: 520-293-3198
Fax: 520-293-3192
(www.darksky.org)

FATAL LIGHT AWARENESS PROGRAM (FLAP)

FLAP works "to safeguard migratory birds in the urban environment through education, research, rescue, and rehabilitation." Formed in Toronto in 1993, FLAP works especially to convince the owners of skyscrapers to turn off unnecessary interior and exterior lights during spring and fall migrations. These lights can draw migrating birds off-course, causing them to circle the lighted towers until dropping from exhaustion or colliding with the buildings. FLAP's work has spread to such cities as New York, Chicago, and Detroit.

FLAP
Royal Bank Plaza, Lower Concourse
PO Box 20, Toronto, Ontario, Canada, M5J 2J1
Telephone: 416-366-FLAP
(www.flap.org)